Younger Me: You Are Free

Younger Me: You Are Free

Interior design: Devyn Maher
www.doodles.blue

Published by:
NyreePress Literary Group
Fort Worth, TX 76161
1-800-972-3864
www.nyreepress.com

ISBN print: 978-1-945304-73-6

Library of Congress Control Number: pending
Categories: Non-Fiction / Memoir / Self-Help / Christian
Printed in the United States of America

Dedication

I would like to dedicate this book, first of all, to my husband, Jim. When we met and got married, I was still a royal mess. But, through his love and determination, he helped me become the person I am today. By believing in me and never giving up, he has been a special gift that I will forever cherish.

Secondly, I would like to dedicate this book to my children: Alora, Sarah, Zillah, Jayla, Nathan and my bubby, Isaac. Through life, trying to figure out where I belong, and through all the emotions I faced, my children have always loved me unconditionally. That love has kept me going in so many ways.

A special dedication to my faithful friends who have believed in me and supported me, especially to my best friend, Becky. She has been an amazing side kick in the process of finishing this book! I am truly grateful to be surrounded by such beautiful people that have helped me become who I am today.

Contents

Introduction

This book has been in thought for many years, but several things have kept me from starting this adventure. First, there was the lie that I am not smart enough to write a book. Then, I had thoughts of reliving the past and hurting the loved ones who were to read this. But, I am confident that God will use what I've witnessed to help and encourage you in your life too.

Over the years, and after life experiences, I have matured in my Christian walk and understand that people don't willingly go around hurting others and allowing bad things to happen. I have learned where the real fight begins and how to overcome. Through my experiences, I hope you will be able to understand how to captivate your identity in Christ and overcome what has been done to you or what you may be going through now. In Ephesians 6:12, it says, "For we wrestle not against flesh and blood, but against principalities, against powers, against the rulers of the darkness of this world, against spiritual wickedness in high places."

Understanding this verse will help you with the healing process. In Ephesians 1, Paul writes a powerful prayer, and this is also my prayer for you as you embrace your own journey to freedom. Verses 18-21 in this chapter are so powerful. Please take the time to meditate on them. Remember, God has a mighty plan for you. The enemy wants to keep you bound. Push through any feelings you may have, and keep seeking, until you receive your healing.

Ephesians 1:18-21

"[18]The eyes of your understanding being enlightened; that ye may know what is the hope of his calling, and what the riches of the glory of his inheritance in the saints, [19]And what is the exceeding greatness of his power to us-ward who believe, according to the working of his mighty power, [20] Which he wrought in Christ, when he raised him from the dead, and set him at his own right hand in the heavenly places, [21]Far above all principality, and power, and might, and dominion, and every name that is named, not only in this world, but also in that which is to come."

In this journey, you will see some of the obstacles I have encountered, and the mentality that was embroidered in my thoughts—how I thought ending my life was the only way out. BUT GOD! Although there were several incidents I encountered, I am going to share some that have stuck with me over the years. I did not grow up in a Christian home. I never was taught about faith. But God saw fit to pull me out of the miry clay. Now is the time for me to share my story and pray you, or someone you may know, can find freedom and overcome. As Peter said, "God is no respecter of persons" (Acts 10:34, KJV).

Before we get started with my journey, I want to share some tactics the enemy may use, or has used, to keep you from pursuing the life God has for you. We will start with what I like to call the Dangerous D's: discouragement, deception, defeat, doubt, diversion, delay, and depression are a few things that may hinder your healing and/or your ability to overcome the afflictions you have endured.

Let's break down each of these Dangerous D's:

Discouragement: Clouding your thoughts, causing you to look at your problems rather than God. Colossians 3:2 – "Set your affection on things above, not on things on the earth."

Deception: Satan's most successful tool. He is the father of lies. Ephesians 6:11 – "Put on the whole armor of God, that ye may be able to stand against the wiles of the devil."

Defeat: Makes you feel like a failure and no good. Hindering you in going forth with God's plan. Romans 8:37 – "Nay, in all these things we are more than conquerors through him that loved us."

Disbelief: Makes you question if you are good enough and question God's plan and truths. Jeremiah 29:11 – "For I know the thoughts that I think toward you, saith the Lord, thoughts of peace, and not of evil, to give you an expected end."

Diversion: Confusion, painting a pretty picture for sin, trying to keep you from righteousness. 2 Timothy 2:7 – "Consider what I say; and the Lord give thee understanding in all things."

Delay: Causing you to put off something so it never gets started or completed. Proverbs 12:24 – "The hand of the diligent shall bear rule: but the slothful shall be under tribute."

Depression: Feeling low or having lost enthusiasm or hope. Hebrews 11:1 – "Now faith is the substance of things hoped for, the evidence of things not seen."

This book is about freedom, how I overcame by the grace of God, and how I learned His truth about who I am in Christ. In this book, you'll learn that we have an adversary plotting against us to destroy us. Understanding there is a spirit realm and an earthly realm was the beginning of freedom for me. Additionally, I came to understand that people just don't go around hurting other people. They are tormented by the enemy, living in a lost world where they know no better.

My desire is to help show others how to make sense of all of this. I want to help them see that they don't have to live a life of bondage. Those who have been hurt and those who hurt others have one thing in common: they are trapped in bondage.

Through my story, I am going to share how bondage can be broken, how you can overcome, and how you can be free! I want you to finally be able to grasp the path God has planned for you. I get so excited when I think back and see where the Lord took me from and where He has placed me today. We all have a story, and your story may be just like mine, or similar. Your story may not resemble mine at all. But, your story is one that needs to be heard and shared too. Several of us are living in a prison created by the enemy, being held in bondage because the enemy makes us feel like we are alone. That is a lie. We are not alone. We are never alone. He likewise will make you believe that no one understands.

It has taken sixteen years for me to have the confidence to share my story. My first attempt caused me to have a nervous breakdown. It was still very painful to reopen the wounds. Therefore I put off writing this book for over a year. My inspiration was renewed by sitting in two different church services the same week. One service, on a Tuesday evening, was at my friend's church. Women meet once a month there for amazing worship and a special word from the speaker. I did not go expecting God to reopen the desire to share this story of mine. Although I was encouraged, and wanted to break open my book again, I was still hesitant. But, when God is ready, He gives us what we need. The following Sunday, while our pastor was away, a good friend of mine was sharing the message that morning. He was speaking on scars, and how our scars have a message.

I knew God was speaking to me. Telling me that it was time. So, I went to the altar for prayer. Like I told him, sometimes when the wound opens, it hurts. Nevertheless, I opened the wound and dug right in. I have to say, this time around, I am seeing things in a whole new light. My past is painful, but God!

Back to the age of five, I can remember countless ongoing cases of abuse. However, it has helped me become the person I am today. I am grateful for this opportunity to share. I made my mind up not to be deceived by Satan's Dangerous D's and pursuing God's plan. I am here to tell you, there is another way! You do not have to settle with deception. You do not have to live with the pain. I did not find the freedom in Christ until I was in my mid-twenties. Being on the verge of suicide with three young daughters—ages three, one, and three months old—was the beginning of me embracing the gift of being set free from all the condemnation that was created.

Every lie that I lived, or was told, was like a brick falling upon me. I was at the point to where my life was consumed by these bricks. I was being smothered, feeling like there was no way out. But God! I began to climb. Climbing through the rubbish I know now that, I am smart enough! I am strong enough! I am good enough! I am worthy enough! I am free! I am an over-comer! So are you!

Luke 10:19
"Behold, I give unto you power to tread on serpents and scorpions, and over all the power of the enemy: and nothing shall by any means hurt you."

Write down the Dangerous D's.

_____

_____

_____

_____

_____

_____

_____

_____

_____

_____

How do each of the Dangerous D's affect you?

_____

_____

_____

_____

_____

_____

_____

_____

_____

_____

_____

Steps you can take to overcome each.

_____

_____

_____

_____

_____

_____

_____

_____

_____

_____

I know this is going to be an emotional journey, as I have tears filling my eyes just thinking about it. I know there are several of you who are struggling with similar situations. As real as the hurt is, the same real freedom awaits you. The battle is real. You don't have to accept defeat. You don't have to live a life of confusion. There is a way to escape the pain. As a young girl, I fought against the spiritual darkness unaware! Through it all, God was always at my side fighting for me. Now, I can embrace the victory and share it with you. Exodus 14:14 says, "The Lord shall fight for you, and ye shall hold your peace."

As I shared in the beginning, many are not aware of the spiritual side of why people do the things they may do. Ephesians 6:10-12 explains so well about the spiritual realm. "10 Finally, my brethren, be strong in the Lord, and in the power of his might. 11 Put on the whole armour of God, that ye may be able to stand against the wiles of the devil. 12 For we wrestle not against flesh and blood, but against principalities, against powers, against the rulers of the darkness of this world, against spiritual wickedness in high places."

Emotions can be another tactic the enemy may use to hinder you from pressing forward to a life of freedom in Christ. Before we get into my story, I would like to reflect on some emotions that I went through over the years. Now and again, we may experience certain emotions, and often experience them unaware. Occasionally, some that go through different types of abuse or rejection are oblivious to their daily reactions. At times, we are not aware of how some of these hidden emotions affect us. Often, I was in denial and not aware that I was affected in my everyday life by these emotions. You may have, or currently be dealing with, many of these feelings.

Section 1

Section 1

Chapter 1:
Anger

In this chapter, I want to start with anger. Having gone through several different types of abuse—including emotional, physical, mental, and sexual—anger was one emotion I had to deal with regularly.

Getting mad over the littlest things, and even over imaginary things, was common for me. Children naturally trust adults. Especially adults who are family or close friends of the family. When one of these trusted adults crosses the line and violates you, most children think it was their fault. Generally, they will also think it is acceptable because they have trusted a friend or family member in your loved one's circle. Once you realize it was wrong, anger may set in. This was my case. I did not understand the abuse I went through, nor did I view it as wrong, as a child. My abusers were family and close friends of our family.

When you have been abused, you have to get to a place where you are not blaming yourself. Understand that, no matter who hurt you or what you were told, it was not your fault. One reflection that gets overlooked is that the enemy was behind this abuse you encountered. Now that the abuse has ended, the enemy will use our emotions to keep us grounded in the appalling situation. If you are still going through abuse, know that it is not appropriate. Most importantly, it is not your fault. In this book, my prayer for you is that you will experience and grasp the freedom in Christ by overcoming the emotions and situations that have besieged you.

Unaware, I suffered from anger. Denial is something often carried by someone that has dealt with trauma. You may feel like you are not struggling, but ask yourself, do you have spurts of hostility, annoyance over simple situations, or snapping over little things? Are you agitated easily? You will think you are responding in a normal manner, but little things may trigger you to act from your hurt. Living in such anger creates a darkness and a cloud, so that at times, you are not even aware of your actions. I became miserable in that anger. I was a very snappy woman. I was always on the edge. The enemy will use these things to keep us from finding our joy! Happiness is a medicine all in itself! The enemy knows that.

"A merry heart doeth good like a medicine"
(Proverbs 17:22, KJV).

"The thief cometh not, but for to steal, and to kill, and to destroy: I am come that they might have life, and that they might have it more abundantly"
(John 10:10, KJV).

Anger held a huge part in my life for so many years. Being angry truly hindered my joy. It is very hard trying to shine your light for Jesus when your joy has been stolen because you are angry. I would have strangers approach me at my workplace asking me why I looked so mean. Therefore, focusing on what my outward appearance looked like, helped me to examine my actions. I want people to see the joy in me. I am so very blessed.

Use this page to journal the anger you had or currently face.

_____

_____

_____

_____

_____

_____

_____

_____

_____

_____

_____

_____

What are some steps you can apply to overcome?

_____

_____

_____

_____

_____

_____

_____

_____

_____

_____

_____

Now and Future Goals.

_____

_____

_____

_____

_____

_____

_____

_____

_____

_____

_____

_____

Chapter 2:
Trust

Upcoming chapters will go into greater detail of certain situations I encountered over the years. Understandably, you will see why trust was another emotion I had a hard time overcoming. There is a betrayal like no other when someone you trust takes advantage of you, and when loved ones lie to you. That may very well cause one to be confused. You begin to ask yourself, "Is this right? Is this wrong? Did I do something I should not have? Why did he/she do this? Why me?"

From the age of five to my adult life, several loved ones broke trust with me. As I got older and realized that those hurting me were wrong, and it was not my fault, I struggled with knowing who I could trust. Living this damaged life, I walked around anticipating someone to wrong me. Who was going to hurt me next? Seemed like the ones I loved the most were the ones I got hurt by the most. Until I found healing from those situations, I had a guard up. I would not allow myself to get too close to people. I was tired of being hurt. I depended on others to help fill a void and mend my brokenness. That only led me to more hurt. I did not even trust myself. If only I had known where my deliverance was. If only—that is another question we are taunted with. We can't live with the 'what if's' and 'whys' we withstood. Asking ourselves these questions does not change what happened. Here and now, we go forward, not looking back. If the enemy has you looking back, that makes it that much harder to move forward.

> "Brethren, I count not myself to have apprehended: but this one thing I do, forgetting those things which are behind, and reaching forth unto those things which are before, [14]I press toward the mark for the prize of the high calling of God in Christ Jesus"
> *(Philippians 3:13-14, KJV).*

> "It is better to trust in the LORD than to put confidence in man"
> *(Psalm 118:8, KJV).*

I am grateful that I found the true peaceful path. I am thankful that God will use the pain I went through to help you and many others. It has taken me years to trust myself and have the confidence to share.

Trust is something that I still struggle with. I have been hurt by so many. When that cycle continues, you just want to stop letting people in. Through prayer and trusting the Lord, I have learned to look at people through the eyes of Jesus. Some want to focus on the bad that people exhibit. I choose to focus on the good. There is good to see in all.

Use this page to journal any trust issues you may have.

_____

_____

_____

_____

_____

_____

_____

_____

_____

_____

_____

_____

What are some steps you can apply to overcome?

_____

_____

_____

_____

_____

_____

_____

_____

_____

_____

_____

_____

Now and Future Goals.

_____

_____

_____

_____

_____

_____

_____

_____

_____

_____

_____

_____

Chapter 3
Rejection

I believe we all have a natural desire to be loved and accepted. In my childhood, I dealt with a lot of insecurity because of how I was raised. Rejection was one emotion that tormented me every waking day. Growing up, we moved around a lot. We did not have a fancy home or fancy things. We didn't even own a vehicle. I got teased by my peers. I was not popular in grade school, middle school, or the earlier years of high school. Some kids can be so mean. For some reason, I was an easy target. Certain youth could spot the smallest detail out and have their fun with it. For example, my mom would buy me white socks only. My peers saw that I only wore white socks. They would laugh and make fun of me in gym class. I know it's really silly, but that was something that really bothered me. These actions from my classmates caused such an insecurity within me.

At times, walking down the hall, it felt like the students were laughing and making jokes towards me. Some clearly were, but not all did. Rejection had already set in my mind. Therefore, it was an insecurity I faced daily by not feeling good enough. The white socks were not the only thing I was made fun of for. I literally had maybe three pairs of jeans. Due to that, my peers made fun of me over that as well. Having to wear the same pair of jeans more than once in a week, I was creative in how I wore them. Tweaking my style was not that difficult. Back in the early 90's, rolled jeans was a popular trend. Say on Monday, I would wear my jeans normal. Then, on Thursday I would roll them, trying to trick the other kids. But, that didn't work. It seemed like an endless battle. Some may say, "Wow, that is really silly. Just kids being kids." That may be so, but the enemy used that bullying and turned it into a big deal for me. Creating such a wall, that I felt all were against me. One thing I want you to see is, no matter how big or small a situation may seem when one is going through it, they are still affected by it in different ways.

Bullying affects so many—especially our younger generations. It certainly does not help with the insecurities and rejections that I faced daily. Altogether, I wanted to disappear, but there was nowhere I could hide. I felt as if all these emotions on the inside were just as transparent on the outside. There was no one I could trust. Not even my own family. The feeling of rejection was so evident to me, no matter where I was. I could be at school or at home; regardless, the rejection did not discriminate. However, feelings of rejection are one of the enemy's tactics to keep us from knowing our self-worth. If he can get us to feel like a loser, then we are not operating in our fullness—in the fullness God has designed for each and every one of us. Our Father in Heaven has birthed many gifts in every human life. Although Satan is the enemy, he is far from stupid. He knows what he is doing. He knows what he is trying to keep us from. His agenda is focused on keeping us from knowing the truths we have in Christ. One truth being that we do not have to live in the bondage created by Satan. He is trying to keep us from operating in the gifts that God has given each of us.

"For he (Satan) is a liar and the father of lies"
(John 8:44, KJV).

I think rejection is one of the hardest emotions to overcome. Being rejected made me feel less than what I was. For so many years of my life, before Christ and after receiving Christ, I strived for acceptance from others. When I was rejected, it hurt. But, God has shown me that, once I accept myself and know who I am in Him, what others think, say, and/or do against me doesn't matter. I am His! I matter to Him. He wants us to love ourselves and see who we are in Him.

Use this page to journal any rejection you may have or currently face.

_____

_____

_____

_____

_____

_____

_____

_____

_____

_____

What are some steps you can apply to overcome?

_____

_____

_____

_____

_____

_____

_____

_____

_____

_____

Now and Future Goals.

_____

_____

_____

_____

_____

_____

_____

_____

_____

_____

_____

_____

Chapter 4
Inferiority

Inferiority is an emotion that has affected me through-out my childhood, teen years, and several years of my adult life. At a young age, I developed an inferiority complex. I had parents who did not have their stuff together, as many would say. Due to an absent, alcoholic father and neglectful mother, their actions created in me a very low self-esteem. With my dad not being around, and the hurtful things my mom would say to me, I did not think very highly of myself. When you think of a child, most kids strive to make their parents/relatives happy. I can see the joy in little ones' faces when an adult they adore is pleased with them. No matter how good I was, or the things I tried to do to make my mom happy, I never met the standards of a good daughter. Feeling like a loser is a way for the enemy to keep us down. If we are feeling low about ourselves, how can we open up to receive something good from someone?

These destructive thought patterns are such a hindrance in our mind. That is where the battle festers. The enemy will fill our minds with untruths of who we are, while using the people we love to make us feel like the lies he is telling are real. These thoughts and feelings held me captive for so long, I did not see who my true self was. This is why it is so important to get to know who God is, and read His Word. His truth is who we are.

> "For the word of God is quick, and powerful, and sharper than any two-edged sword, piercing even to the dividing asunder of soul and spirit, and of the joints and marrow, and is a discerner of the thoughts and intents of the heart"
> *(Hebrews 4:12, KJV).*

Finding verses like the one above, and declaring God's promises over your life, will help you start believing in who you really are. You are the body of Christ. We need to train our minds to think on good things and true things.

> "Finally, brethren, whatsoever things are true, what-soever things are honest, whatsoever things are just, whatsoever things are pure, whatsoever things are lovely, whatsoever things are of good report; if there be any virtue, and if there be any praise, think on these things"
> *(Philippians 4:8, KJV).*

My husband now, Jim, has helped me overcome being inferior. Growing up and having to fend for myself had me in a place where I had to depend more on me than anyone else. Now, Jim was the first man in my life to love me, but I had a hard time accepting that. He helped me to see that I was not alone, and I learned to lean on him. This was a new sense of freedom, having someone I was able to confide in, trust, and share with.

Use this page to journal any inferiority you may face.

_____

_____

_____

_____

_____

_____

_____

_____

_____

What are some steps you can apply to overcome?

_____

_____

_____

_____

_____

_____

_____

_____

_____

_____

Now and Future Goals.

_____

_____

_____

_____

_____

_____

_____

_____

_____

_____

_____

Chapter 5
Anxiety

For me, my anxiety started to attack me at the age of twelve. I was completely alone in my thoughts and surroundings. I carried a torturous fear of losing the ones I loved so dear. I always feared the worst to happen. It is safe to say, I did not have a normal upbringing, mentally. Anxiety hit me in the form of OCD (Obsessive–Compulsive Disorder) which is a mental disorder where people feel the need to check things repeatedly, perform certain routines repeatedly (called "rituals"), and/ or have certain thoughts repeatedly. Most people are unable to control the thoughts or activities for more than a short period of time. I did not know this then, but I clearly know now. The thoughts I was taunted with were all lies from the enemy. They were so real to me at the time. Daily, I was fighting a battle in my thoughts. I feared greatly that something terrible would happen to my mother or brother if I did not perform these rituals. It was an endless struggle. I would complete one routine, then the lies would bombard my mind to the point where I would have to do more and more.

From being a young girl, at the age of twelve, to an adult at the age of twenty-four, the OCD rituals affected me. I spent twelve long years dealing with these agonizing thoughts, unaware of my true self. I was completely confused about what was real or fake, lies and truth; the world around me was a fog. Suffering from this disorder made it very difficult for me to do average, everyday tasks. Likewise, it made it difficult to be normal. I knew people saw the way I acted, and the rituals I would do. It was not something I could hide. Dealing with rejection made this anxiety worse. I was literally terrified 80% of the day—constantly in fear of what could happen. One of the greatest burdens I carried was that, in my mind, I was not allowed to share with others why I was acting out the actions I did. In my mind, if I was to tell, then something bad would happen. These thoughts hit me daily. The anxiety took control of my life.

I ask myself now, "What did my family think? What did my husband (at that time) think?" The OCD was a secret I carried day-after-day for over twelve years—not sharing or confiding with anyone. It was just me, my thoughts, and the lies from Satan. In the back of my mind, I wondered if they knew. I'll explain more about the attack of OCD when I share my story. In this verse, we learn that the serpent (Satan) can deceive us. At times, when we are not taught or don't know Jesus, our minds become corrupt.

"But I fear, lest by any means, as the serpent beguiled Eve through his subtilty, so your minds should be corruptedfrom the simplicity that is in Christ"
(2 Corinthians 11:3, KJV).

Every day, we are in a battle. We have an enemy that is against us. We need to prep ourselves and be ready. The best way to be ready is to have the whole armour of God on! I have heard people say, first thing in the morning, put your armour on. I am telling you, DON'T take it off! Put on your belt of truth and breastplate of righteousness, shoes of peace, shield of faith, helmet of salvation, and the sword of the spirit—one of our greatest gifts, honor, and privileges is prayer. Keep your armour on. Just because you go to bed at night, does not mean the enemy won't bother you.

> "[10]Finally, my brethren, be strong in the Lord, and in the power of his might. [11]Put on the whole armour of God, that ye may be able to stand against the wiles of the devil. [12]For we wrestle not against flesh and blood, but against principalities, against powers, against the rulers of the darkness of this world, against spiritual wickedness in high places. [13]Wherefore take unto you the whole armour of God, that ye may be able to withstand in the evil day, and having done all, to stand. [14]Stand therefore, having your loins girt about with truth, and having on the breastplate of righteousness; [15]And your feet shod with the preparation of the gospel of peace; [16]Above all, taking the shield of faith, wherewith ye shall be able to quench all the fiery darts of the wicked. [17]And take the helmet of salvation, and the sword of the Spirit, which is the word of God: [18]Praying always with all prayer and supplication in the Spirit, and watching thereunto with all perseverance and supplication for all saints"
> *(Ephesians 6:10-18, KJV).*

Most of the anxiety I experienced dealt with the battle that was ongoing in my head, which lead to frustrations and depression. But, the more that I learned about the spiritual realm and drawing closer to God through His word, the more He taught me how to captivate my thoughts. Taking my thoughts captive and analyzing them helped me see what was true and what was false. The enemy will bombard our minds, causing us to become fearful, leading us to anxiety. Knowing this is one of his tactics helped me overcome!

Use this page to journal the anxiety you may face.

_____

_____

_____

_____

_____

_____

_____

_____

_____

_____

_____

What are some steps you can apply to overcome?

_____

_____

_____

_____

_____

_____

_____

_____

_____

_____

_____

_____

Now and Future Goals.

_____

_____

_____

_____

_____

_____

_____

_____

_____

_____

_____

_____

Chapter 6
Feeling Alone

Unfamiliar with how to deal with my feelings, I still deeply cared for others, especially my mom and brother. Feelings of confusion were undeniable. It was difficult to understand what had perplexed my thinking. No matter what, I was terrified, confused, and struggled for a sense of belonging. I do believe at times, even as young children, we may not know what we are looking for, but the need is still there. With all these things, another to add was that I did not have the privilege of friendships. I am sure that my insecurity played a part in not being able to make many friends. Don't get me wrong, growing up I had a few friends, but not many. One of my flaws was that I had major trust issues. Not knowing my self-worth, I focused on the ones that were against me more than the friends that were for me. As I ventured into my adult life, my friend situation remained the same. No, I don't blame everyone else. Although children, teens, and even adults, can be misunderstood, I was just as guilty for pushing people away. I saw myself how I thought others viewed me.

I did not fully understand how any kind of relationship worked. Now that I am older, and have a clearer understanding, I love this verse in the bible: "A friend loveth at all times"

(Proverbs 17:17, KJV). Friends are a special treasure we hold. I have learned that Jesus is the greatest friend we could ever have. God loves us so much that He has given us friends to help and comfort us. Going through trials, no matter what age you are, friends are someone God created for each of us to have. The enemy will work to shut out people, to leave you feeling that you are fighting this battle alone, but God's word confirms that two are better than one. He has never planned for us to be alone in this world.

> "Two are better than one; because they have a good
> reward for their labour"
> (*Ecclesiastes 4:9, KJV*).

Several areas of my life were hindered because I felt the need to constantly prove myself. I believed I was someone that I was not. There was a daily battle happening in my mind. Deep down, we know who we are, but the thought process and lies that constantly invade our thinking become like a tug-of-war. Separating the facts from lies causes such confusion that, at times, we don't know what to believe. Then, we are left trying to figure out why and trying to make sense of things. Although, knowing why and making sense of things is not what I needed at that time. What I needed was to be delivered. Unsure of how to be free of this bondage was one of the things keeping me trapped. I was not only troubled in my thinking, but the bondage also clouded several areas of my life.

Struggling with trying to keep or maintain a healthy friendship, I also had to deal with being violated by loved ones I trusted. This only added to the confusion. I may have seemed normal, or may even have portrayed myself as if nothing was going on, but things were happening on the inside. Slowly or suddenly, my self-worth was being chipped away. I was too young to even realize that a part of my innocence was stolen. You know, I have heard comments in my past about, "Oh they are just kids. They really don't understand," but children know and feel so much more than adults give them credit for. To me, one of the sweetest verses in the Bible is, "And Jesus called a little child unto him, and set him in the midst of them, And said, Verily I say unto you, Except ye be converted, and become as little children, ye shall not enter into the kingdom of heaven. Whosoever therefore shall humble himself as this little child, the same is greatest in the kingdom of heaven" (Matthew 18:2-4, KJV).

This is Jesus explaining how little children are. For one to think a child is only a child, and situations do not impact their lives, is a mistake. Every time a child goes through sexual, emotional, or physical abuse, their self-worth, piece-by-piece, chips away. A child may not understand what is happening, but the enemy is feeding them with the emotion of feeling unworthy. It's like you always have to be on guard; as if you have to live in defense mode, defending yourself and feeling rejected by so many. These are things children should not have to concern themselves with. I wanted to be wanted. I wanted to be accepted.

Was there ever a time when you viewed yourself as others made you feel?

_____

_____

_____

_____

_____

_____

_____

_____

_____

How do you see yourself now?

_____

_____

_____

_____

_____

_____

_____

_____

_____

Know that each of us are fearfully and wonderfully made, and we are new creations!

"I will praise thee; for I am fearfully and wonderfully made: marvelous are thy works; and that my soul knoweth right well"
(Psalms 139:14, KJV).

"Therefore if any man be in Christ, he is a new creature: old things are passed away; behold, all things are become new"
(2 Corinthians 5:17, KJV).

Write down seven positive things about yourself. When you begin to feel low about yourself, or your mind drifts, think on these things again.

_____

_____

_____

_____

_____

_____

_____

_____

_____

_____

_____

_____

_____

_____

Section 2

Section 2

Chapter 7:
Now, My Story Begins

I will share with you a little history about the first eleven years of my life. My mother and father divorced shortly after I was born. My mom liked to party and have her fun. We had lots of people in and out of our home most days. My dad was hardly seen while we were growing up. My mom never really had nice things to say about him. Due to his absence, I grew up thinking that he never really cared for me either. I do not have many memories of my dad. The one that has stuck with me is when I was about four or five. My mom was "out" and we were with a sitter. My dad came and kidnapped my brother and me. We were only little kids then, so I don't know what the real deal was between my parents. Looking back now, I think my dad missed us, and in his mind, that was the only way to spend time with the two of us.

I remember traveling to this motel. I was really young, so the details are a bit fuzzy, except for this one. Not really sure why this memory sticks out, but I remember having breakfast with him and my brother at a pancake house across from the hotel. We were enjoying our time together. That was one of the first moments I had with my father. We were with him a couple days, then he returned us home. I do not think my dad was being spiteful with his action here. I felt he was genuine in his motives. Don't get me wrong, my father was not a model guy. He was absent most of my life. Popping in here and there. He too had his demons that he fought with. My dad was a big alcoholic and user. He had been in trouble with the law numerous times. My mom did not like my dad much.

Regardless of his lifestyle and actions, growing up without a dad was hard! I believe every little girl has a special connection with their daddy. I was robbed of that. Nonetheless, I did have stepfathers growing up, but they did not fill the void of not having a dad. It certainly was never the same. As a young child, we moved a lot from Maryland to Northern Virginia, back and forth. My brother and I spent a lot of time by ourselves. Sometimes we were off outside doing normal kid stuff, hiding out in our bedrooms, or watching our favorite cartoons. We did have several different people living with us off and on.

One particular guest, who had to stay with us, was my uncle on my dad's side. I was about six years old at the time, and he was fourteen. I was just a little girl, not knowing any difference between right and wrong. Late at night, my uncle would get in bed with me. He would talk softly to me. In his whispers, he would tell me what to do to him while he did things to me. I never did tell my mom. To be honest, he was my uncle; I trusted him. I thought this was normal behavior. This opened up other doors, and I found myself acting out in an adult-like manner with other family members and friends.

When I was eight, my mom and her friends were having a party, playing cards, and doing their own thing downstairs. I had a "boyfriend," and we decided we were going to have sex. This kind of behavior I grew up around, thinking it was normal. Now let me clarify: I don't think we really had sex—just went through the motions of it. However, during our experimenting, this other little boy interrupted us. Then, he went downstairs to tell on us. My mother and the other adults came to see what we were doing. She asked me if this had ever happened before. I casually told her about my uncle. She was angry by what I told her, but that incident did not change anything. I was still a confused little girl trying to find her own way in this messed up world.

A couple years after that, my mom met my last stepdad. This guy was different. My mother was dependent on men. She had several boyfriends while I was growing up. My mom finally got with a guy who had his priorities straight, and we started to live a normal life when he was home. He was a truck driver, so when he was out on the road, my mom would continue her party life. But when he was home, things were nice. My stepdad's job caused us to move around a lot. One particular job took us to North Carolina.

Up to this point, I was just a young girl, unsure if right and wrong meant anything. Going along with what I was told and trusting those that I should not have. While we were living in North Carolina, the spiritual battle within me had begun. I still remember what my bedroom looked like. It was bright, the last room on the left. Of course, I had the teeny bop posters on my wall. I had bunk beds and a desk. One specific detail I remember is, on my desk, there was a little white Bible. I am certain that the Bible was given to me at birth from my grandmother. Although I never knew what this Bible really was, I knew it was special, and I treated it like a treasure.

My brother knew that it was special to me. Being that typical brother, he liked to rattle my nerves. Thus, he would come in my room and pile stuff on it, making jokes, trying to get me mad. When his friends came over, they would play around and play their games along with my brother. At that time in my life, I did not understand why I felt such a connection to this book. But, there was something there. I now know why. I was clueless about what the contents of this book consisted of. Nevertheless, I knew this book was important. One thing I don't understand is why I was never taught what was inside of this amazing book. I do recall sitting on my top bunk wanting to read it and know about it. Starting in Genesis, I began reading. I cannot remember how far I got, but I know it wasn't but a few chapters.

Our family was rather small. In our home, it was only my mom, step dad, brother and myself. My grandmother was very active in our lives. We would mainly see my uncle—my mom's brother—aunt and cousin during the holidays. At home or on holidays, I cannot recall a time when we prayed as a family or even attended church together. The only thing I remember about any church talk was my mom saying, "I was forced to go to church as a child. I will not force my kids to go."

One thing I have learned in this thing called life is that church is a great place to be for fellowship. Also, it is a place to learn how to fight against the enemy and daily battles. Most importantly, it's a place to learn about God's unfailing love. A place we find hope where we thought there was none; we now have a hope in Jesus. Unfortunately, my mom was blinded from these blessings. Satan had her comfortable in feeling like she didn't need a church and her children did not need to go either. She was not against us going. At one point, our neighbors— who were very active in church—invited my brother and me. They had a son and daughter the same age as us, so we went. I cannot say I got the whole church thing, and fully understood what was going on, but I do believe seeds were planted. To look back, I can't help but acknowledge how awesome our Father in Heaven is. God was always there, watching out for me. At my fingertips, I had His truth the whole time. All those exhausting days and endless nights that I felt so alone, I really wasn't. He was always there comforting me. I now realize that all the pain I had gone through made my God sad too. The enemy knew God had a plan for my life. So, the enemy worked on destroying that plan. But God. I needed that guidance to help show me the way. Satan knew that and put up as many roadblocks as he could to keep me from embracing my true self and who I am in Christ. While I was being distracted with the busyness of life and circumstances, I was not completely able to focus on the plan that God had for me.

"For I know the thoughts that I think toward you, saith the Lord, thoughts of peace, and not of evil, to give you an expected end"
(Jeremiah 29:11, KJV).

"Be sober, be vigilant; because your adversary the devil, as a roaring lion, walketh about, seeking whom he may devour"
(1 Peter 5:8, KJV).

What are some of the distractions in your life (the past or present) that are keeping you from going to that next level in your walk with Christ?

_____

_____

_____

_____

_____

_____

_____

_____

_____

_____

_____

What next steps are you ready for?

_____

_____

_____

_____

_____

_____

_____

_____

_____

_____

_____

Chapter 8
As a Child

As a child, I remember having a huge heart. I had a very strong love for my family! There wasn't anything I would not have done for them. At this point in my life, we were living in Charlotte, North Carolina, and I was twelve. This was the time that the spiritual attacks started to affect me. Torturing thoughts started to hit me hard. As in the beginning, I shared about suffering from Obsessive–Compulsive Disorder (OCD) (To re-cap - OCD is a mental disorder where people feel the need to check things repeatedly, perform certain routines repeatedly—called "rituals"—and/or have certain thoughts repeatedly. Most people are unable to control the thoughts and activities for more than a short period of time). Common activities include hand washing, counting things, and many more. My greatest fear was the thought of losing my mother and my brother. The fear of something bad happening to them was constant.

These thoughts invaded my mind, trying to convince me that the lives and safety of my loved ones were my responsibility and left in my hands. These thoughts relentlessly tormented me every day. Some days, it was a constant never ending thought. Thoughts that had me believing that in order to keep my family safe, I had to perform these rituals. The rituals started out as me having to turn the lights off and on repeatedly. Then, they moved to touching things a certain way and a certain number of times. Whenever I came to a doorway, I would stop, then have to do this side-stepping thing—moving my left foot to the left side of the door frame and my right foot to the right side of the door frame—numerous times in a row. My foot would go left, right, left, right, left, right, until I felt the release to stop. The struggle was so real. Not only was the struggle real, it was exhausting. The thoughts were so powerful in my mind that I honestly felt if I did not perform those rituals, something bad would happen to my family.

It was the only thing that felt real in my life. My family saw me acting these rituals out. Instead of seeking help for me, they would laugh and make fun. I could not explain to them why I was doing the things I was doing. Now, I was not only struggling with this mental illness, I was feeling a great rejection from my loved ones that, in my mind, I was trying to protect. Just imagine as a little child carrying a burden like that. I did not know the power of our Almighty God at that time. I did not know how to seek help for what I was going through. I did not know how to practice this verse:

"Come to Me, all who are weary and heavy-laden, and I will give you rest. The rest that comes from the Lord is such a peaceful, reassuring rest" (Matthew 11:28, KJV).

Use this page to lay some of your burdens down. What have you struggled with that you can only find rest in the Lord?

_____

_____

_____

_____

_____

_____

_____

_____

_____

_____

_____

Chapter 9
A Mom's Choice

My mother was not like most mothers. She did make sure our needs were physically met. However, she was very dependent on help from men. Unfortunately, my stepdad had divorced my mom. We moved from North Carolina back to Maryland. When I was fourteen, there was a life changing incident that really took a toll on me. It was on a Saturday night, the same weekend as Mother's Day. The night started out with me going to my neighbor's home down the street to babysit. My mom was working overnight sitting with an elderly man. It was approximately 3 am when I left from babysitting. When I got home, my mother's boyfriend was up waiting for me. I had come in from the back door, which was also our kitchen entrance. I sat down at the kitchen table, maybe for a drink or snack before bed, but I honestly don't really remember why. My mom's boyfriend had come around the corner with nothing on but a robe. As he made that turn, the robe was completely opened in the front. He did not have any clothes on underneath.

I had a very uneasy feeling, so after talking to him for a few minutes, I decided to go to bed. Moments later, he lightly knocked on my bedroom door. I laid there in my bed pretending to be asleep. When I did not answer, he welcomed himself into my bedroom. He began by saying to me, "Your mother has been working a lot lately." Then, he made me get out of my bed. We were now standing at the foot of my bed as he started to force himself on me. The crazed look in his eyes was so unsettling. The way his hands touched my body was frightening. I did not want to be doing the things he was asking me to do. Some of the sexual things he told me to do, I'd never even heard of. Being confused and frightened, the only thing I could think of was, how am I going to escape this? I asked him several times to let me go to the bathroom.

Finally, after about a half hour of his exploitation, I was able to convince him to let me go to the bathroom. He finally agreed, but would only let me go under one condition, that he go with me. So, I complied. Knowing that my brother's bedroom was right across from me, I had a plan. He grabbed me by my hand, and we walked out of my bedroom. Instantly, as we approached the hallway, I placed my back against the wall and dropped to the ground. I then started to scream loudly for my brother to hear. He took his hand above my head and grabbed me by the hair. He had lifted me up off the floor trying to keep me silent. In the midst of all the commotion, my brother had woken up. My mom's boyfriend went into my brother's bedroom to persuade him that I was having a bad dream, and he was only trying to calm me down. I took this opportunity to bolt to the bathroom. I slammed and locked the door.

For a brief moment, I felt relieved. Then, my mind was saturated with what just happened. I was terrified, not knowing what to do next. Feeling confused, one thought fluttered through my mind .... he is going to finish what he started. I knew I had to escape. In fear, I took off running out of the bathroom, down the hallway, through the kitchen, out the back door, and headed to the neighbor's home I had been babysitting at. In the process of arriving at their house, I ran and ran in the pitch-black night. I was terrified of not knowing what would happen next. I am thankful my neighbors were still awake and answered my cry. Frantically, I shared with them what had just happened.

They instantly called the police. While we waited for the police to come, the mom took me to her bedroom to help calm me down. She wanted me to feel safe. As I sat on her bed, she started to brush my hair. Endless strands of hair were coming out from where he had grabbed me, pulling me up from the floor. He was arrested that early morning. The police contacted my mother. A couple days later, I was faced with a very hard decision. This would have to be the most difficult part of my story. Like I mentioned, my mother was very dependent on men. But, with her dependence on men, she had asked me to say that what happened was only a dream. She wanted her boyfriend to come home. She said we couldn't make it on our own. I loved my family so much and would do anything to keep them happy. Watching my mom go through this hurt made me sad. Since my mother asked me to do this, I did not think it was wrong to lie at that time. On account of, I went to that courtroom to say I was mistaken. Then, I lied and told the court I was having a dream that night. Of course, I regret it now. Even though I was fourteen, I still was only a child blinded. Confused with the difference between right and wrong, love and hate, I did what I thought I had to do. I honestly don't know the difficulties my mother went through with this situation. I know she believed me and knew he attacked me. She was scared of not being able to support our household without his help. She later explained to me she didn't think I could live with myself for sending him to prison. Either way, it was still a difficult time to pass.

He was released from jail and moved back into our home. Having him walk through our doors again was such a difficult feeling. I did not want him to be back. He continued to abuse me in other ways and invade my privacy. Their bedroom and the only bathroom we had were side-by-side. Her closet wall was right against the bathroom wall. He had peep holes and would watch me undress and shower. One of the most private rooms in our house, and I was terrified to go in. Because for me, it wasn't private. I would shove the peep holes with toilet paper, but he would remove it or create another. I did not feel safe and lived scared most of the time—kind of like being a prisoner trapped in my own home.

He would go into my room when I wasn't there. I put paper in between the door and door frame to mark if he had gone in my room while I was in school. Several times, I would come home and that paper would be laying on the floor. I am not sure what he did in my room, but one thing I know is he would take my clothing. In his own way, he would taunt me. I can still recall the sick way he stared at me. It was a very disturbing time. We then found out that he was a known pedophile. Months later, the police came to our house questioning us about another incident he was involved with. They had arrested him, and this time, he went to jail. While the police searched our house for evidence, that is when they found some of my items in his private area down in the basement with his semen on them.

Already suffering from the obsessive thoughts—OCD—after this trial, they started to hit me hard. I developed a hand-washing ritual, along with the others, that I would perform several times within a day. These rituals consumed my life. In all this, I felt so alone. Your story may be similar to mine. Your story may be totally different. I want to express that no matter the story, experience, or situation, God cares about all our hurts, no matter how big or small! Twenty-six years later, I am still affected by it, but I have found healing. I am grateful that I understand now about the spiritual realm. I honestly pray for my attacker. I pray he will know the love of our mighty Father! I pray that he will find freedom and know that forgiveness can be his too. A forgiving heart will help experience true healing.

"If we confess our sins, he is faithful and just to forgive us our sins and to cleanse us from all unrighteousness"
(1 John 1:9, KJV).

"Be kind to one another, tenderhearted, forgiving one another, as God in Christ forgave you"
(Ephesians 4:32, KJV).

Take this time to write a letter to the one or ones that have hurt you. I am not asking you to send this letter to them. Ultimately, that will be your choice. I know sometimes writing out your feelings helps some heal in a different way. It can help you deal with some emotions that may be hidden. Do this in prayer first. Carrying the bitterness that was caused by your situation only hurts you in the end. Many don't feel that the one that caused them pain deserves forgiveness. That allows the enemy to carry a hold over you. Although you are struggling and hurting, the love and forgiveness you give is the key to your healing. I forgave my attackers in my heart. I did not send a letter or see them face to face. But, God knows our hearts. He knows how we feel and is very faithful in helping us overcome.

"O Lord my God, I cried unto thee, and thou hast healed me" *(Psalm 30:2, KJV).*

_____

_____

_____

_____

_____

_____

_____

Chapter 10
The Rebellious Teen

Feeling alone, I tried to find a sense of belonging in alternative ways. I started smoking cigarettes and drinking alcohol at the age of twelve. At sixteen, I started smoking marijuana. The older I got, the harder the drugs I experimented with. I had this delusion that comfort came from those of the opposite sex. I had also become quite the kleptomaniac. That became a different kind of obsession for me. It was a need I felt, an addiction. It did not matter where I was or what kind of store I was in, I had to take something. I would steal cigarettes, ten to twelve packs at a time. I would take gum. One time, I even stole Vienna sausages. If I saw I could get away with it, I took it. The more I got away with thieving things, the more I started to go bigger and bigger. Even as a young mom, I would take the diaper bag in the store and load it with whatever I thought I needed or wanted. I do believe that the OCD played a huge part in this awful habit. Take this, do that, do it again, you need to take more. Constant negative thinking dwelled in my head. It was as if I were living two lives. Whether I was stealing something, washing my hands, or whatever obsession, I felt it needed to be done. The thoughts and rituals were always there, taunting me.

Some knew a little about the real me, but many only knew me depending on what mask I was wearing. In high school, I got made fun of often my freshman and sophomore year. As I mentioned earlier, I never had many friends. When the sexual abuse happened from my mom's boyfriend, I felt some compassion from my peers. They knew about the abuse because there was an article in the paper. Since I was a minor, my name was not mentioned. However, the road I lived on was a private road. Not many families lived on our road. Of course, I was the only fourteen-year-old girl there. Going back to school after that Mother's Day weekend, the students knew I was that young girl in the newspaper article. There was a small period of a "feeling sorry for me" stage at school. But, that was short lived.

The emotional and sexual abuse were not the only types of abuse I encountered. Physical and mental abuse played their part as well. I am not sure where my mom stood in life. Whether she was willing in making her choices or if she felt she had no other option. I love the story about Mary and Martha in Luke 10. We all have choices and there is a way that may not be easy or make sense, but it is right.

> "[38]Now it came to pass, as they went, that he entered into a certain village: and a certain woman named Martha received him into her house. [39]And she had a sister called Mary, which also sat at Jesus' feet, and heard his word. [40]But Martha was cumbered about much serving, and came to him, and said, Lord, dost thou not care that my sister hath left me to serve alone? bid her therefore that she help me. [41]And Jesus answered and said unto her, Martha, Martha, thou art careful and troubled about many things: [42] But one thing is needful: and Mary hath chosen that good part, which shall not be taken away from her" (Luke 10: 38-42, KJV).

My mother was just an unhappy person. I can't say what she thought or felt. All I know is what I felt and the things that were said and done to me. Remembering how she reacted to certain situations, those actions lead me to believe and feel I was a burden. There were several times she had taken her frustration out on me. With her words, her hand, a thick ole' triangle school ruler, and my not so favorite, an old cutting board with fifteen holes drilled in it. I have to say, I do not like those triangle rulers or cutting boards with holes. I was not disrespectful or a rebellious teen growing up, but I did exhibit normal teen behavior. Of course, I tried getting away with those things we did as teenagers. When I got in trouble, normally I would stand still and take it.

Let me tell you why I do not like those triangle rulers. One afternoon, my mother was pretty hot about something. I knew I was about to get it. This time I did not stand and take it, but ran to the corner of my bedroom. Quickly, I got in the fetal position while she took that ruler and wailed on me. Although she was hurting me, I felt I deserved it for whatever reason. Now, that cutting board with fifteen holes. Let me tell you why I did not like that tool of hers. Acting out in my teenage years, my friends and I did that thing where I was staying at my friend's house and she was staying at mine. My friend's boyfriend was having a party, and we really wanted to go. Well, we got told on and my mom came down that hill and dragged me out of the party by my hair. She had her boyfriend drill fifteen holes in that cutting board. She decided to give me fifteen straight forward whacks to the bum. She proudly displayed that thing where we all could see it. Although I did not have much of a relationship with my biological father, I wanted to go live with him after that.

I never understood why my mom got so mad at me for going to that party. She would allow me to drink and smoke at home. But I couldn't understand why she wouldn't allow me to go party elsewhere. Those two physical incidents have stuck with me more so than the others. Physical pain hurts. It is something that you can clearly feel. Verbal attacks are just as painful to deal with. Often, we are affected by the words of others. Whether they say the things they say out of truth or just being mean, it is just as hurtful.

When I was just a little girl, maybe eight or nine, my mom spoke these words to me, "I wish you were never born." That was a very painful phrase that has always stuck with me. I never understood why she would say that to me. Was it out of anger? Did she really mean it? In all honesty, it doesn't matter why she said it. I had thoughts go through my mind, trying to figure out why. One thought I had was, did she say that because I am a girl? My mother always favored my brother growing up. He would annoy me, I would yell at him, and guess who got in trouble. Yes, me! He would do something wrong, and yet I seemed to get the blame. My brother and I are only ten months apart. Despite our petty issues, like getting on each other's nerves, we were close. I feel he tried to look out for me and protect me the best he could. But, he also liked being that annoying older brother too.

It truly breaks my heart to paint this picture of my mom. I did not know this then, but now I realize that she was allowing herself to be controlled by the lies the enemy was telling her. If only someone would have shared the love of Jesus with her. Maybe someone did. I don't know. What if she would have received God's grace? So many what if's! But, that wasn't our story. Even through all that, I still loved and adored my mother. I was somewhat of a caretaker for her. I watched out for her well-being. Countless nights I went into her bedroom, taking the burned-out cigarettes out of her hand. Staring at her chest to make sure she was still breathing. My mom was lost. She struggled with the deception from the enemy.

The thoughts that were embedded in my mom's mind were all lies from Satan. It was the enemy that branded her life with such untruths. Why does the enemy do such things? Well, he wants to keep us from living a life of freedom in Christ! This is why it is so important for born-again believers to go out and be the hands and feet of God. There are many that are stuck in a whirlwind of lies, not knowing what way to go. In the path of the whirlwind, others are affected, being scorned and branded. But with God, there is a way out. We need to be that door to show others.

> "Who comforteth us in all our tribulation, that we may be able to comfort them which are in any trouble, by the comfort wherewith we ourselves are comforted of God" *(2 Corinthians 1:4, KJV).*

> "Wherefore comfort yourselves together, and edify one another, even as also ye do"
> (1 Thessalonians 5:11, KJV).

> "Every word of God is pure: he is a shield unto them that put their trust in him" *(Proverbs 30:5, KJV).*

What are some of the lies the enemy has told you?

_____

_____

_____

_____

_____

_____

_____

_____

_____

_____

Write your plan of action on overcoming and taking back what the enemy stole from those lies.

_____

_____

_____

_____

_____

_____

_____

_____

_____

Chapter 11
Masks We Wear

In this chapter, I will share how things began to change my life. I was able to see things from a different perspective. My junior and senior year of high school, I attended a vocational school. I liked the mask I wore there! I was popular! My junior year, I enrolled in the Printing and Publishing trade. That is where I met who would become my best friend, Selena. She was the first person that I clicked with and could let more of my real self be seen. She never knew everything, but it was nice to finally have someone I could call a friend. Someone I could share some things with.

It is so sad the roles we play in life. At times, you may feel you have to hide part of yourself. I think we do that because we don't understand who we really are. How are we to explain to someone else what is going on, when you can't explain it to yourself? The enemy uses this to convince us to hide our true selves. He wants to keep you in a dark place. When you come across a true friend, and are finally able to share some of your secrets, it can be somewhat of a release. You may even begin to see things in a different light. I may not have shared with Selena everything that went on, or was going on in my life, but she could tell. She saw things for herself, and she was a true friend. I can proudly say that almost thirty years later, we are still friends.

My senior year, I was the homecoming queen, president of the student body, and editor of our yearbook and newspaper. For the first time, I felt somewhat important. People saw a side of me that made me feel like I was someone. I was liked. It felt good! But that was just a part I played in that thing called my high school life. These years in high school were an escape for me. I was able to be free and experiment with what was in the world. These were the best two years of my life so far. For the first time, I was having fun. For the first time, others looked up to me. For the first time, I felt a sense of escape from the things that had happened to me. A lot of great "firsts" for me. However, it did not change what was going on within myself and the daily struggles that festered in my mind.

We become fake, putting on the smile and pretending like everything is okay! God has called us to be true to ourselves! God does not want us to wear a mask and be fake. He wants us to be free! He wants us to be who He created us to be.

"So God created man in his own image, in the image of God created he him; male and female created he them" (Genesis 1:27, KJV).

"Henceforth I call you not servants; for the servant knoweth not what his lord doeth: but I have called you friends; for all things that I have heard of my Father I have made known unto you" (John 15:15, KJV).

"But I fear, lest by any means, as the serpent beguiled Eve through his subtilty, so your minds should be corrupted from the simplicity that is in Christ" (2 Corinthians 11:3, KJV).

What are some of the masks you have worn?

_____

_____

_____

_____

_____

_____

_____

_____

_____

_____

_____

Chapter 12: Looking for Love in All the Wrong Places

Although I carried such a deep love for my mom and brother, I truly didn't understand what love was really about. But, it was something I longed for. One thing that I find so strange is how, although I didn't "know" God, I would still ask Him to take me out of this world. I was a miserable human being. Feeling lost, lonely, scared, and unimportant. A young woman with no value. I had been robbed of my identity. I didn't even know who I was. Circumstances had me in a dark place. I did not think very highly of myself. I allowed myself to be used by my family, friends, and men. I had no self-worth—which led me to unhealthy relationships with those of the opposite sex.

You know the saying, looking for love in all the wrong places. On the weekends, my friends and I would hang out at this under twenty-one club. We would dance and drink non-alcoholic strawberry daiquiris. It was there I met my first real boyfriend. I was sixteen, and he was a grade ahead of me and so dreamy. That night, we connected and started dating. It was really nice to finally have someone pay attention to me and make me feel like I was someone. We had gotten really close. My mom even allowed him to move in. After a few months of being together, he proposed to me. And of course, I said yes.

After he graduated, and I was a senior, he became very controlling. He did not like me going anywhere or doing anything without him. He then became abusive. We were together about two years. In all honestly, considering the history in other relationships, I believed that this behavior was acceptable. When my fiancé and I ended our relationship, I was eighteen. That was the beginning of me losing control of myself. Falling into temptations with other men, drugs, and alcohol. The bar scene was something I was familiar with. You could even say it was a place where I felt comfortable. Growing up, before I was old enough to be in school, my mom and her friend would go and shoot pool. My friend and I would color in our coloring books at a bar booth.

At the age of sixteen, I was a regular in the bar scene. At times, I was even served alcohol. By the time I was eighteen/ nineteen, I was getting into clubs. The meaningless sexual relationships I got involved in added up. It was one guy after another. Those guys never cared about me. They just took advantage of my weakness. Drugs were even becoming more common to me—constantly desiring any other feeling. At this time, I was lost in it all. Finding comfort in all the wrong ways. If you have found yourself in a similar place, or may even be there now, know there is a better place to be. I now understand that the enemy had me in the wilderness, going in circles to keep me from the One who could offer me true comfort. Which reminds me of Matthew 4, when the enemy tempted Jesus—Verse 1. "Then was Jesus led up of the Spirit into the wilderness to be tempted of the devil."

One of the most comforting chapters in the word of God is Psalm 91. I can't help but share these promises and comfort. Please take the time to dissect this word. Breathe it in and believe it for yourself.

"¹He that dwelleth in the secret place of the most High shall abide under the shadow of the Almighty. ²I will say of the Lord, He is my refuge and my fortress: my God; in him will I trust. ³Surely he shall deliver thee from the snare of the fowler, and from the noisome pestilence. ⁴He shall cover thee with his feathers, and under his wings shalt thou trust: his truth shall be thy shield and buckler. ⁵Thou shalt not be afraid for the terror by night; nor for the arrow that flieth by day; 6 Nor for the pestilence that walketh in darkness; nor for the destruction that wasteth at noonday. ⁷A thousand shall fall at thy side, and ten thousand at thy right hand; but it shall not come nigh thee. ⁸Only with thine eyes shalt thou behold and see the reward of the wicked. ⁹Because thou hast made the Lord, which is my refuge, even the most High, thy habitation; ¹⁰There shall no evil befall thee, neither shall any plague come nigh thy dwelling. ¹¹For he shall give his angels charge over thee, to keep thee in all thy ways. ¹²They shall bear thee up in their hands, lest thou dash thy foot against a stone. ¹³Thou shalt tread upon the lion and adder: the young lion and the dragon shalt thou trample under feet. ¹⁴Because he hath set his love upon me, therefore will I deliver him: I will set him on high, because he hath known my name. ¹⁵He shall call upon me, and I will answer him: I will be with him in trouble; I will deliver him, and honour him. ¹⁶With long life will I satisfy him, and shew him my salvation"
(Psalm 91, KJV).

Please take the time to reflect in some areas you have had trouble, or are having trouble overcoming. Where may Satan be keeping you captive?

_____

_____

_____

_____

_____

_____

_____

_____

_____

_____

_____

How can you apply Matthew 4 and Psalm 91 to your situation to help you overcome?

_____

_____

_____

_____

_____

_____

_____

_____

_____

_____

Chapter 13
That Phone Call

At the age of nineteen, I had met the man I was going to marry and have a family with. He was an experienced guy, also nine and a half years older than me. He had already been married to three different women before we met. But, he walked the walk and talked the talk, and knew how to work it with the ladies. How did it all get started? Well, I was home alone one afternoon when our phone rang. Barely getting to the phone because I was getting out of the shower, it was him on the other end. It was at that moment over the phone, we made our first date arrangements. Our date consisted of meeting at one of the bars. Afterward, we had taken some beer up to my apartment. He stayed with me that night. We were up until the next morning getting to know each other.

The bizarre thing was, that night was our first date. He stayed that night and the next, and the next, and so on. That was the beginning of our relationship. We lived a simple life. Neither one of us had many responsibilities. Our schedule consisted of hanging out at the bars, then most nights we would bring the party back up to our apartment. We would stay up most nights, drinking and playing video games with my mom. Of course, we would then sleep most of the day. Essentially, we were getting lost in our troubles and having no accountability. Living this kind of lifestyle, I started to see things that really bothered me. He would get too comfortable with the other ladies. Although we were a couple, he liked his freedom in that area. Not wanting to lose him, I ignored my jealousy and dealt with it. It bothered me a great deal but, I was afraid of being alone.

Despite him being married in his past, he was my first adult relationship. Manipulation was one thing he was good at. I saw things he would do and heard things he would say. Aside from that, he was good at convincing me that the things I saw and heard weren't what I was seeing and hearing. I just went with the flow. He was not good at being faithful, but one good quality he had was making sure I was taken care of. I never really had someone take that kind of interest in me. That part was nice for a change. I know he did have a special place in his heart for me.

In life, I feel like most of us are looking for that someone to take an interest in us. Often, we seek this in the wrong ways. Many times, we don't seek it at all. Sometimes it just happens. All along, we have always had someone who cares for us.

That was the beginning of our life together. This was the area of my life where drugs started to play a bigger part. Up to now, I was only smoking marijuana. I had gotten hooked on 'poor man's cocaine'. I was an addict. I remember going to the bathroom at the bus station and at bars to snort this drug. This was a new way for me to get lost. That is one thing that many do not understand. Satan will use things in life to make us feel better. But it never lasts long, he will eventually lead you to bigger, more dangerous things. Being caught up in this trap, there is no satisfaction. Therefore, you are left to search and search. You find yourself grabbing on to whatever it is that "feels good", whether it is good or bad for you.

We often get scared, not knowing what to do or where to go. But, Isaiah 41:10 tells us, "Fear thou not; for I [am] with thee: be not dismayed; for I [am] thy God: I will strengthen thee; yea, I will help thee; yea, I will uphold thee with the right hand of my righteousness."

"Casting all your care upon him; for he careth for you"
(1 Peter 5:7, KJV).

"Cast thy burden upon the LORD, and he shall sustain thee: he shall never suffer the righteous to be moved" *(Psalms 55:22, KJV).*

"Humble yourselves therefore under the mighty hand of God, that he may exalt you in due time: Casting all your care upon him; for he careth for you"
(1 Peter 5:6-7, KJV).

What are some things you need to cast at the feet of Jesus?

_____

_____

_____

_____

_____

_____

_____

_____

_____

_____

_____

What is keeping you trapped?

_____

_____

_____

_____

_____

_____

_____

_____

_____

_____

_____

_____

Chapter 14
Stranded

I was living in Maryland with my mom in our apartment. My mother and I still did not get along well. In 1996, the east coast had a big blizzard. I remember it well. It was the first time my mom had kicked me out of our apartment. I walked several miles in this blizzard, to my brother's apartment to have a place to sleep for the night. Unclear on how many days I was away from home, I eventually went back. This was not the only time my mother kicked me out of our home. Shortly after returning home, my mom had thrown my ex and I out again. This time, we really did not have any place to go. I was stranded and left out on the streets to fend for myself. It was very embarrassing, having to ask someone if we could crash at their house. So, for as long as we could, we made what we could work. Whether it was finding a dark unused closet it the apartment complex my mom lived in, or walking the streets until we found a place to rest our heads. One night that sticks out from all the rest, was a night we had slept on the porch of an abandoned house. I was too terrified to go inside, so we decided to crash on the porch for the night. Finally, friends of ours welcomed us to stay with them.

Shortly after that, my mom made the decision to move back to Virginia. She wanted us to go with her. I was very skeptical and scared about going. We discussed it and decided to go with her. Our lifestyle continued in Virginia. It was always partying, drinking, and drugs. One day, my mother and I got into an argument. At this time, I was nineteen years old and finally reaching my breaking point with her. She was standing at the top of the stairs. I was approximately three or four steps below her. In the midst of us arguing, she grabbed me by my hair and pulled me up the stairs. Without thinking, for the first time ever in my life, I hit my mom back. I honestly cannot say I am not proud of that decision. She looked at me and told me to get out.

Once again, she kicked me out of our home. But this time, I was in an area where I did not know anyone. Stranded again, in an area that was unfamiliar to me. Being distraught I left, not knowing what to do. As I sat at a picnic table waiting for my boyfriend to join me, I held my head down low, wondering where to go from here. He had stayed behind for a short bit to talk to my mom. Nothing changed, we were officially on our own to conquer this new journey that was before us.

In times of feeling stranded or alone, here is an awesome verse of amazing comfort.

"Have not I commanded thee? Be strong and of a good courage; be not afraid, neither be thou dismayed: for the Lord thy God is with tee whithersoever thou goest" *(Joshua 1:9, KJV)*.

In times of struggle, I find listening to worship music or opening God's word enlightens me. Write down a few positive ways you can enlighten your day when feeling alone.

_____

_____

_____

_____

_____

_____

_____

_____

_____

_____

_____

_____

_____

_____

_____

_____

Chapter 15
A New Journey

Not far from where we were was a cheap motel. That was our first place together. Although the circumstances were not the greatest, I thought it was so cool to be staying there. This was a new journey we were facing—the first time I felt like an adult. Whereas I was feeling scared and unsure, I was happy to be out on our own. We had made the choice that this time, we would not go back. We were going to move forward and work on a life together. It was very tough in the beginning. We stayed in different motels. Then, a female friend of his allowed us to stay at her house. This was tough for me, considering he had issues with not remaining faithful. One night at her house stands so clear in my mind. We were fighting, I had left for a while, and when I returned, he was in her room… in the dark. With his smooth talking, he convinced me that he wasn't doing anything wrong. Besides that, where was I going to go? I did not have any friends in this new area, and I felt like I needed him. Therefore, I overlooked things and chose to believe his smooth talking. Needless to say, I was extremely happy when we were able to get out of "his friend's" home.

Our first official place on our own was an efficiency motel

with one of his co-workers. This was another exciting step for me. One precious moment at that time of my life were two little additions we had. We had two kittens, c-a-t (Saddy was her nick name) and boots. They were my babies. After living there approximately two months, we were able to get our very first apartment. How exciting this was! His co-worker moved in with us for a short while. For our jobs, we would work together often in factories. He was good at maintaining work and taking care of us.

Although I was not aware of God's love, and the promises He had for me during this time in my life, this verse is a great reminder of His love towards us in times of trying to figure things out.

"But they that wait upon the Lord shall renew their strength; they shall mount up with wings as eagles; they shall run, and not be weary; and they shall walk, and not faint"
(Isaiah 40:31, KJV).

As you adventure into your relationship with God, and make new decisions in your life how can you 'wait upon the Lord?'

_____

_____

_____

_____

_____

_____

_____

_____

_____

_____

_____

_____

_____

_____

_____

Chapter 16
Then, There Were Three

It was a few months later we found out we were going to become parents. I was so excited. From the age of sixteen, I wanted to have a baby. I had this void in my life and desire just to be wanted. I wanted someone to love and to love me back. Knowing I was going to be a mother was extremely exciting for me. The factory I worked at didn't need me any longer so I was now staying home. This gave him the time to make other friends and meet people. When I was four months pregnant, he left me for another woman. I was terrified. How was I going to make it on my own with no job and a baby on the way? I didn't know how to take care of myself. I certainly did not know how to be an adult on my own.

Living a life of rejection and not measuring up, I absolutely did not think I could make it on my own. I thought I needed him to survive. Being alone in this apartment and not having any income coming in, the electricity eventually got turned off and things really started to fall apart. When things got really bad for me, he ended up coming back. At this point, I was almost seven months pregnant. We moved into a trailer together and got married. I was terrified of being alone and having a baby on the way; it seemed like the only way I could survive. Therefore, I was relieved that I was not on my own any longer. Our marriage was awful! We fought a lot, and he had become abusive. He too was angry often. Most of the time, he took his anger out on me. And other times, he would destroy things in our home that we had worked hard to get.

On top of all this, he was still unfaithful. Feeling trapped, I dealt with it, because I did not want to be alone. There were moments of my life, that I thought I was living a lifetime movie. The evil that I would see in his eyes was terrifying. The accounts I share with you are only a small portion of the bondage and torment I faced. With stating that, I would love to take a moment and say how thankful I am. Even though I was unaware of who God was, and the mighty power He holds, I am so very thankful that He was with me through those times.

At age twenty-one, I had my first baby! A beautiful baby girl! Wow! I held her in my arms and looked at how perfect she was. I was in love! Something changes when you become a mother. Something unexplainable. All I knew was I wanted to protect her from anything and everything. Becoming a mother, I started to see things in a different light. I looked back at my life, and the things that were allowed to happen to me as a child, and wondered, how? Up until now, I had a casual relationship with my mom. No matter what happened, I had that desire to have a mother-daughter relationship.

However, looking at Alora, my first baby girl, something else changed inside of me. I now looked at my mom in a different way. I started to break off relationships with everyone. One of the first connections I broke was with my mom. I slowly distanced myself from her. Alora's dad was working and barely coming home; so, it was just me and my daughter. We were living in a small trailer when Alora was born. I did everything I could to keep her in my sight. I had a little white bassinet that I would lay her in. If I was in the kitchen I rolled her in there with me. We were inseparable! When I had to use the bathroom, I rolled her back in the hall with me too. Having her was the first bit of happiness I had ever experienced. I held on to this happiness tight.

No matter what you are going through and how you feel, know that God is good and someone you can trust.

"The Lord is good, a strong hold in the day of trouble; and he knoweth them that trust him"
(Nahum 1:7, KJV).

How can you open up and allow God into your life more?

_____

_____

_____

_____

_____

_____

_____

_____

_____

_____

How can you lean on Him more to trust Him?

_____

_____

_____

_____

_____

_____

_____

_____

_____

_____

_____

Chapter 17
Our Growing Family

Approximately two years later, we were now living in West Virginia. I was pregnant with our second child. The morning I found out I was pregnant, I was so excited! I ran from the bathroom out into the living room to share the news with Alora. We were blessed with another little girl, Sarah. Sarah was such a calm, sweet blessing. It brought me great joy for Alora to have a baby sister. My labor had begun around 9:00 a.m. We were living out in the middle of nowhere with no phone. This was the year 2000, therefore social media was not a big thing yet for our family. My husband was due home earlier in the morning because he had been working the night shift. Sadly, he had a habit of not coming home after work.

I had gotten up that early January morning with contractions and no sign of him. Around 3:00 p.m. I decided to drive to the country store and call his mother. Thankfully, she was able to get a hold of him. Approximately 6:00 p.m. he came home, and he was drunk! I loaded the car with our overnight bag and tucked Alora in her car seat. He started to drive us to the hospital. After riding with him five to ten minutes, I had him stop the car so I could drive the rest of the way. He was too intoxicated to be driving and was all over the road. We lived about forty minutes from the hospital. Once we arrived, I took Alora into the hospital. We got everything set up, awaiting my baby girl to come. We were not at the hospital long before she came soaring into the world. I was very thankful we got there when we did!

Shortly after her birth, I was pregnant again with our third daughter, Zillah. I was not aware of God and His plans then, but I look back and smile because He knew what He was doing. Alora and Sarah were so close and like best friends. Zillah was being breastfed, therefore took a lot of my attention. But, the four of us had such an amazing bond. Being filled with so much joy, it was an honor to be a mommy to three amazing little girls. Be that as it may, it did not take long for the obsessive thinking to start to focus on my daughters. This really affected me in a major way. To live in daily fear of losing your child is torturous. My daily rituals had gotten worse. The lies the enemy was telling me were, "If you don't do this, then something bad will happen." I would wake in the mornings and couldn't wait to go back to bed. The thoughts were so hard to bare. I lived in such fear day-after-day, that I would hardly allow the girls to go outside and play. I did not like to go in public, and when I did, I would hold tight to the girls. I remember having Alora hold on tight to the shopping cart while Sarah and Zillah were in the cart. On a daily basis of being at home, if there was a crack in my curtains, I would fold over the edges so no one could see in. I lived in awful fear that I would not even allow them sleep in their own rooms.

I can happily say that I was no longer involved in drinking or drugs. I had even quit smoking cigarettes. The disturbing thoughts weighed heavy on me in several ways. Although I had these precious children, I still desired my life to be taken. Being chained to these acts each day drained me. Physically and mentally, I was at the end of my rope. I felt as if I had no control. Being a mom to three adorable daughters, at the age of twenty-four, and having a husband that was abusive and a cheater, along with these constant thinking patterns, I did not know which way I was going. My husband was an alcoholic and violent. There were several days in a week that were not good days.

The fighting and arguing was constant when he was home. I think back to some of the situations the girls and I faced, and thought it was just a coincidence that we made it out okay. However, I now know that it was the hand of God protecting us. When my husband would get angry, the girls and I were put in harm's way. For instance, when we were still living in the trailer—and you know how tiny trailers can be—he kicked Alora's car seat into the air. The car seat barely missed her head and landed inches from her. As time went on his anger grew even worse. When he got mad, if I was near him, I would get hit. If I wasn't within reaching distance, he would throw things or come after me.

Alora was in a high chair one evening. He was angry and decided to throw a full can of soda at me. Missing her head by inches, it hit me in the arm. I was so grateful it missed her. It didn't matter what I was doing or where I was, if he was angry he would act out. While pregnant, he had come after me when I was showering. Ripped open the shower curtain and started to release his frustration on me by wailing me in the back. I did what I could to protect the baby by turning into the corner, face first and hunched over.

We were living out in the country, with no way to communicate with anyone unless they stopped by our home. I did not know anyone here except for our landlords. I dealt with being alone, not having any friends to share what I was going through. I was forced to just deal with what was going on.

Although I was not a believer at the time I became a mom, I knew my girls were a gift. Even though I was messed up, I loved them and wanted to do what I could to give them a good life. I now know that these precious babies were a gift from God.

"Every good gift and every perfect gift is from above, and cometh down from the Father of lights, with whom is no variableness, neither shadow of turning" *(James 1: 17, KJV).*

Through some of your tough times, what is the one thing (or things) that has helped you stay strong?

_____

_____

_____

_____

_____

_____

_____

_____

_____

_____

How can you let God in to help?

_____

_____

_____

_____

_____

_____

_____

_____

_____

_____

Chapter 18
Breaking Point

Being stuck with the abuse I faced daily, I was so scared on so many different levels. Twelve years had passed since the taunting OCD invaded my life. Through the years, the thoughts and rituals had only grown deeper. There was nothing I could do to ease my uncontrollable thoughts. At this point, I was feeling helpless and wanting it all to be over. This memory stands so vividly—the day I reached my breaking point. I was standing in my kitchen, washing my hands, (one of the OCD rituals) several times—feeling so done! As I was in front of the sink, I took a glance over to the left. On the counter was a bottle of prescription pills. I had just given birth to Zillah, therefore had the pain medication that the doctors had prescribed to me. I heard this voice within my head say, "There is only one way out," gearing my face towards those pills.

At the same time, I felt my body shift and something holding my arms as I heard these words within my head, "Those girls need you." At that moment, I felt so confused and torn. I was ready to be done with having these feelings and thoughts. I did not want to carry out another day living in these rituals. After twelve years of the tortuous thoughts, I had finally reached what felt to be the end. I was ready to admit myself into a psychiatric hospital. I had even considered going into a hospital to get help. But, I couldn't leave my baby girls. For the first time since suffering from OCD, I knew it was finally time to do something. Finally having the courage to share with my husband the trials I have encountered through these OCD attacks opened the door to my first steps towards freedom.

Although my husband was not the greatest of husbands, he knew something that I didn't know. He did not exhibit a life of knowing Christ, but he had encountered knowledge of our risen Savior before he met me. In the midst of my breakdown, he says to me, "You need to read the Bible." I have to be honest, this was not the response I thought I would get. Up to this point, I had accepted this miserable, unhappy life I allowed the enemy to build. I was ready for a change. I wanted to be happy and enjoy my life. I was willing to do anything to be free and normal. My husband went to the Christian bookstore and bought a study Bible and another book to help me with the overcoming process. I was ready to jump in and see change.

I did not know what to expect. This was all new to me. I did not grow up with, nor had I been taught to have, a relationship with God. I was not aware of the freedom and truths the Bible contained. I certainly had no idea of how the spiritual realm operated. As I read this book, my eyes began to open. I started to see that I was allowing myself to be the enemy's puppet. I realized that the thoughts I had been having over the years were lies told to me by the enemy. The rituals that I performed daily were all part of Satan's game.

It is very hard to put into words the feelings, emotions, and thoughts I was experiencing. For the first time, I felt hope. Many that have gone through similar situations as mine, received help from doctors, medication, therapy, and more. I feel honored to have had the right guidance at that time to show me an easier path to reach freedom. I am glad that I was open to allowing God to work and reveal the light to me. No, it was not an overnight experience, but it was the beginning. I do believe this was a miracle. The chains I carried daily were some big chains. As I dug deep into that book and read God's word, those chains began to break.

Now freedom starts! Was it easy...no, not at all! But was it worth it? Absolutely!!! I embrace the change and am grateful for where God has brought me and what He delivered me from! I still have moments, but I do not allow myself to dwell or live in them! True freedom comes when you can Praise God for the deliverance and see where the real battle comes from, the enemy.

Ironically, as I was going through this deliverance period, my husband and I separated weeks after I began my freedom journey. He told me he wanted to sow his oats and get it out of his system. Although I was angry with him for cheating on me, I did not want him to leave. I was terrified of being alone. I was finally feeling good and excited about having a normal life, then this happened. It put me in a depression, but I knew I had to keep going. I had three beautiful blessings that were count-ing on me. Alora and Sarah were like best friends. That made me happy knowing they were happy and had each other. Zillah really helped me with feeling needed and keeping my focus as a mom. She was only three months old when her father left. She was a breastfed child, therefore while feeding her, I felt how much she needed me. I felt how needed I was. It was extremely hard transitioning over to being a single mom. It was not in our plan to separate. After all, how many oats can one sow?

Undoubtedly, I was feeling like I was at my end. Many let downs and many times of feeling alone. But, at this point, I began to see hope and feel something different. I was now learning of our Savior and how to become free.

> "Then they cried unto the Lord in their trouble, and he saved them out of their distresses. He brought them out of darkness and the shadow of death, and brake their bands in sunder"
> (Psalms 107: 13-14, KJV).

At your breaking points in life, what helped you get past them?

_____

_____

_____

_____

_____

_____

_____

_____

_____

_____

_____

How can you allow God in to help with any chains that you feel are still attached?

_____

_____

_____

_____

_____

_____

_____

_____

_____

_____

_____

Chapter 19
History Repeats Itself

Throughout our separation, he knew I was trying to get my life on track with God. The girls and I started attending a local church, and I would study at home. Since he was familiar with the Bible, he would use certain scriptures to benefit him and keep me under his thumb. As I was a newbie in learning about the Bible, I was easily persuaded by what he would tell me. He was not living at home with us but would come often to have me fulfill my "wifely duty" considering we were still married. he would tell me I could not be with any other man according to the Bible. I believed the things he would tell me. Although we were separated, I still felt trapped living a life with him, under his conditions.

We were working on getting back together until I found out he was having a baby with another woman. I see how ridiculous this seems now, but at that point in my life, I could share him with other women and overlook things. I did not like sharing him. I did not feel like I had a say, but I couldn't accept the fact that he had started a family with someone else. Becoming a mother and starting a family life was something that I viewed as precious. Having to share him in that way was something that was too difficult for me to do at that time. Therefore, I went ahead and pursued the divorce.

Many would think, *divorce, now you don't have to live under his rules any longer.* I did not know how to be a bold, confident woman in Christ yet. I was learning that He created me to be those things. I still allowed myself to be told what I could do and could not do according to him. Even though we were not living together, and were legally divorced, he still had control over my life. I was still living in a prison. It was as if he watched my every move. He would always tell me that he was my husband, and I could only be with him. To be honest, I was not really interested in being involved in another relationship. In life, you have two kinds of adults. Adults who become replicas of how they were brought up and repeat the process of neglect and abuse to their children. Then, you have the adults that make their minds up that they do not want to be that kind of parent. I did not have all my stuff together, as they say, but I knew I wanted to give my kids a good life and protect them. I was focused on growing my relationship with God and becoming a good mother to my girls.

As time went on, I did start dating a guy that I worked with. Mostly when the girls were with their father, my co-worker and I would see each other. My ex-husband did not approve of this at all. I began to see that not-so-good side of him again. He would hide outside of my house and watch. Somehow, he knew when I was with my new boyfriend.

I was living with a friend of mine at this time. One night, I went out on a date. My friend was home watching our kids. While I was out, my ex-husband decided he was going to stop by my house. After realizing I was not home, and I was out with a guy, he became furious. Reaching inside my kitchen cabinet, he had begun to shatter my dishes all over the floor. He took my television set and threw it out in the yard. The study Bible he bought me... he tore it apart. I came home to a huge, unnecessary mess. Needless to say, the relationship with my co-worker did not last long.

At this same time, he was involved in a relationship, and they had two children together. I didn't understand how it was okay for him to move on and have an extended family with someone else, but I couldn't even date. I was still tied to him. Manipulation was one thing he was good at. I would believe anything he said. He had a way of convincing me from day one. I think back to the way I allowed things to go and the control I allowed him to have over me, and just wonder, *what in the world were you thinking, Lutricia?*

To make our situation even more complicated, there were several times I would babysit for him and his girlfriend, so they could go out. One occasion, I was at their house. When they had gotten home, he was livid about something that had happened while they were out. I am not sure what was going on or what happened, but I was laying on the couch in their living room with Zillah on my chest. He came over to me while I was laying there and decided to take his frustration out on me. He started wailing at my head as Zillah was only inches away. I was able to turn and lay her on the couch. Then, I got up and ran to the back room where his girlfriend was. I thought maybe she could help, but I was wrong. I jumped on the bed, huddled in a ball while he beat me from behind. In the midst of all the chaos, we ended up in the kitchen. His girlfriend, who feared for my life heard me screaming. She ran into the kitchen to help me as he had a screwdriver, saying: I have to do this.

When he was done, I went back out to the room where the girls were. He had gone outside and blocked my car in with his car and a riding lawnmower. When he came back in, he sat on the couch across from me. The look in his eyes was like looking in the Devil's eyes. While he stared at me with that taunting look, he held his belt in his one hand slapping it against his other hand, just staring. I was terrified. I felt like I was in a lifetime movie at that moment. Once he passed out, I gathered my babies, put them in the car and finagled it out of the tight spot he put me in. Reverse, forward, reverse, forward—time after time until I eventually got my car out.

I then headed to the hospital. The hospital already knew what the deal was, but of course, they could not do anything because I lied and said it was not domestic abuse. It makes me so sad to know the number of women who go through this. They lie to take up for the one that is hurting them. It is time to seek help and be strong. If you are, or if you know someone who is in an abusive relationship like this, please get help. I realized many things that night. With a slip of his fist, he could have hit my daughter. At the force of his punches, that would not have been good. A wrong hit to the head, he could have done more damage to me. When one is so angry and loses control, the strength they are capable of is unspeakable. Please know, you or someone you may know, there is a way out. Feeling stuck, being afraid, and not being confident in who you can be is keeping you in an unhealthy and dangerous place. There is a way out! Seek the one who gave it all for you!

> "He shall redeem their soul from deceit and violence: and precious shall their blood be in his sight" *(Psalm 72:14, KJV)*.

> "He delivereth me from mine enemies: yea, thou liftest me up above those that rise up against me: thou hast delivered me from the violent man" *(Psalm 18:48, KJV)*.

I highly recommend getting involved with other Christian people. Most spirit-filled Christians will be there to help and direct you. Without condemnation!

> "Bear ye one another's burdens, and so fulfill the law of Christ" *(Galatians 6:2, KJV)*.

"A man that hath friends must shew himself friend-ly: and there is a friend that sticketh closer than a brother" *(Proverbs 18:24, KJV).*

What are some truths you can tell yourself to help you break free of someone else's control?

_____

_____

_____

_____

_____

_____

_____

_____

_____

_____

_____

Chapter 20
Reunited

In the midst of it all, I was reunited with my dad when Alora was nine months old. As I had mentioned earlier, my dad was not in the picture much at all. My brother was getting ready to go into the Marines. Before going to boot camp, he wanted to re-connect with our dad. I have to say, it was a bit awkward at first, but it was also nice having the opportunity to get to know my dad, step mom, and my little sister. They lived in Maryland, and I was living in West Virginia at this time. We would travel back and forth to see each other often. When Sarah was born, she was born with a cyst in her nose. As she grew older, the cyst grew with her. Her doctors recommended surgery to have it removed, otherwise it would continue to grow. When she was seventeen months old, my dad, step mom, and sister came to stay with me for support and to help out. I needed help with the kids; Alora was almost four, and Zillah was just a few months old.

At the time of Sarah's surgery, I was separated from her father. To have my dad and his family come help was a great support for me. Unfortunately, my dad still had some bad habits. My ex had just given me child support before they had come to stay. The night before Sarah's surgery, while we were sleeping, my dad got into my purse and took my child support money.

He left in the middle of the night and drove up to Maryland to buy drugs. I was heartbroken and could not believe my dad had taken this money from me, his daughter. I was more disappointed that this was one more person in my life that I had trusted and loved, that wronged me. My step mom and I took the kids to the hospital together to have my daughter's surgery done.

Sarah's surgery was one of the hardest moments of being a mother I had to face. To watch the doctors sedate her, as she was slowly going in and out, was a terrifying sight. When she fell asleep, the nurses explained how to get to the elevator. Walking out that door was not easy. However, entering the waiting room was one of the first times I was courageous enough to express my Christian faith. I got on my knees in that waiting room and prayed. Praise God, the surgery was a success and all was well.

Considering what my father had done, my step mom was still supportive and active in my life. My dad continued making bad decisions with drinking and drugs, and eventually got caught and went to prison. After being locked up for awhile, my dad started writing me. We started to develop a relationship again. However, my step mom and others had cut ties with him. When it was time for him to be released, years later, he had no one to pick him up. I decided to go get him. After he was released, he lived with my brother for a while. My dad began to rebuild his life, even went to church with me. After some time, my dad and step mom got back together. Our relationship was different this time. It was good.

My father had lived a rough life with drugs and alcohol. Sadly, he had gotten very sick. The doctors only gave him approximately six months to live. But, he made it eighteen months. During that time, my kids and I got to know my dad and love him dearly. Towards the end was really difficult. My whole life, I struggled with not having a dad in my life. Now that I finally got him back, and our relationship was great, I was going to lose him. My step mom called me one night to tell me that he had gone non-responsive. I went to Maryland that night and arrived the next morning. We were only there a few hours, and my dad left to be with the Lord. During his last hours on earth, he could not respond to us, but I sat by his side as his cheerleader. I don't know what he was going through in his final hours, but I sat there and told him over and over, "Go with Jesus, Daddy, go with Jesus." My step mom gave him permission to leave, and moments later, a single tear fell from my dad's eye and he left. Although I don't have my Daddy on earth, I have hope to see him again.

Having the opportunity to build a relationship with my father taught me something. No, he was not the best or perfect dad. But, he was my dad. I learned that forgiveness is truly important. As a Christian, it is our duty to show love, even to the ones that have abandoned us.

"I therefore, the prisoner of the Lord, beseech you that ye walk worthy of the vocation wherewith ye are called, With all lowliness and meekness, with longsuffering, forbearing one another in love; Endeavouring to keep the unity of the Spirit in the bond of peace"
(Ephesians 4:1-3, KJV).

"And be ye kind one to another, tenderhearted, forgiving one another even as God for Christ's sake hath forgiven you"
(Ephesians 4:32, KJV).

Knowing it is not easy to forget the wrong one has done to you, is there a loved one in your life now that you desire to build a relationship with?

_____

_____

_____

_____

_____

_____

_____

_____

_____

If so, what are the results you are looking for?

_____

_____

_____

_____

_____

_____

_____

_____

_____

I encourage you to pray and seek God in helping you accomplish this.

Chapter 21
Hope

Through the many heartbreaks and disappointments this life has thrown at me, God was always there, waiting for me to find Him! God is an almighty God that can and will fill any void in our lives. Although I miss not having a real relationship with my mother, and not having a father figure for most of my life, God has always taken care of me and been there for me. Today, He has blessed me more than I could ever imagine. I know I am not perfect in this world that we live in, but He is faithful and doesn't just leave us! He is and always will be there. Our part is to grab a hold of this truth and run with it. Know who you are. Feelings will lead you down the wrong path and confuse your mind. Knowing who you are in Christ will help you be victorious in any situation.

I highly recommend getting involved with other Christians. Most spirit-filled Christians will be there to help and direct you. Without condemnation! After becoming a single mom of three children, things were really rough at times. I can honestly say that when I found a church family, they helped look after me. When others have the love of Christ in them, the compassion they show is moving. It is our job as Christians to be the hands and feet of Christ. I was shown this through many acts of love from those that God placed in my life. The girls and I lived a very simple life and did not have much money, but God made sure we were taken care of.

Becoming a new Christian, one thing I started to do was tithe. I honestly feel God honored me by my faithfulness in tithing. To give the church ten percent of my income did not seem to be an option for me. I just knew it was something God wanted me to do. So, I did! Can I say it was easy, no! There were times when I got paid and had approximately forty dollars left for groceries and gas to last for two weeks. Again, but God! God always made sure we had everything we needed. Many times, we were given love gifts. I would get into my car after leaving a Sunday service and there would be a box of food on my passenger seat. One Easter weekend, I was surprised with beautiful Easter dresses for my girls along with a special toy. One thoughtful love gift we received, to this day I still do not know who blessed our family with these gifts. I do believe it was members of the church I was going to. One evening, I heard this noise on my front porch. I went out to see what it was, and there were two huge totes. Inside these totes were so many items for me and the girls. From cotton balls to shampoo and special little things for the girls. It was a real blessing. Alora wanted to go to camp one summer, and someone blessed me with the funds for her to go. Anonymously, someone left enough cash in my cup holder for her to go. I could go on with the list of blessings from God's faithful people. Although things were tough, God looked after us, and I knew we were going to be okay. Another little treat that I remember were the .99 cent happy meals every Tuesday night. As silly as that may seem, it was a treat we all looked forward to. They loved it! These small things gave me so much hope.

"Bear ye one another burdens, and so fulfill the law
of Christ"
(Galatians 6:2, KJV).

"A man that hath friends must shew himself friendly: and there is a friend that sticketh closer than a brother" *(Proverbs 18:24, KJV).*

As you began to seek God, what were some of the 'wow' moments you have experienced?

_____

_____

_____

_____

_____

_____

_____

_____

_____

_____

Chapter 22
A New Life

About three years into my new life in Christ, I met my husband now. Up to meeting Jim, my ex was very forceful in destroying any relationship I was interested in. But, something was different with Jim. My ex, for the first time, had started to back off. My first date with Jim consisted of him taking my daughters, his daughter, and myself out for a family fun day. Our day started out at an indoor amusement park. The kids rode some rides and played on the indoor playground. For lunch, we all got pizza. When we left there, he had taken us to the park where the girls fed the ducks and played. It was really the perfect first date. We had so much fun. Jim was really different than anyone else I had encountered.

After dating for a couple months, I experienced something that I had never experienced before, love. I was twenty-eight years old when we started dating. I lived twenty-eight years on this earth not feeling loved by any other person, besides my children. With Jim, I knew he loved me, and it was a feeling I'd never had. Needless to say, we were only dating five short months before deciding to get married. He has been an amazing husband, he and I have grown together in the Lord and seen

God do magnificent things. My relationship with my husband now was proof that any relationship built on God's standards will prosper and be a great one.

I was still on the path of learning who I was in Christ. When I was introduced to God's word and steps to freedom, it was not an overnight deliverance for me. I was going through the emotions of church. Being faithful in attendance. Trying to allow God's word to penetrate through me. However, I would not allow His truth to penetrate. I held on to the lie that I was no good. Come on, I had a mother who did not want me, a father that was never around (until the end) and one failed relationship after another. If my own family could not love and want me, how could this God love and want me? That was a stronghold that took a long time to get over. All these years had passed, and I had been faithful in church and experiencing God's goodness. But, I still had a hard time accepting that God loved me. About a year after being married to Jim, I remember sitting in a church service and it hit me. Wow, God does love me! This was a new beginning for me.

Satan will use what he can to keep you from grasping the whole truth of who you are. So many are unaware of strongholds that the enemy will use to drag Christians down. Often, new Christians will get caught up in the do's and dont's of Christianity. I don't think that is where God calls us. Yes, as Christians we have a particular walk we need to walk, but God does not want us to live every day wondering if we are doing things right. Living each day with, 'we can't do this, we can't do that.' He desires our heart to be pure with getting to know Him, loving Him, and leading others to get to know Him.

The previous chapters are only pieces of my past. Of course, I did not include every situation I encountered. I shared what I felt God lead me to share. I am sure that since you are reading this, you can relate to some of my past experiences. Your past may be similar or very different. These next chapters,

I want to go deeper into the word and share with you some of the truths that helped me separate the real from the fake, and the truth from the lies. Regardless of what your struggles have been, these steps and understanding will help you on your path to a victorious place in Christ!

Understanding that now you may be feeling alone, and deep down you know there is a change that needs to be made, I encourage you to push through and grasp these next chapters. You may have felt alone for so long, but know this, now is the time where you do not have to fight this fight of feeling alone any longer. You no longer have to feel as if you need to figure this life out. Humble yourself before our Almighty God. Seek the help you need that can only come from our Father in Heaven. Getting to a place where you can rest in God, you will see yourself overcoming more efficiently. One misconception people have about God when they are getting to know Him is, they think that God is upset with them. God is not angry with you! That is a lie from Satan. The enemy will bombard you with thoughts of your past, and try to get you to question yourself. For years of going to church I believed the lie, my own mother and family couldn't love me, how could God? The enemy will come at you to make you feel like God is angry, upset and not interested. Know that God is Love and He loves you! He is not mad at you!

> "Trust in the Lord with all thine heart; and lean not unto thine own understanding. In all thy ways acknowledge him, and he shall direct thy paths" *(Proverbs 3:5-6, KJV).*

Take this time to reflect on some of the struggles you currently have and be prepared to lay them at the Father's feet.

_____

_____

_____

_____

_____

_____

_____

_____

_____

Prayerfully ask the Lord to help cleanse your mind of distractions and soak up His love while you embrace His truths.

_____

_____

_____

_____

_____

_____

_____

_____

Chapter 23
This Is Us

As it took me many years to have the courage to share my story with the world, I am now forty years old. I look back on my life and the relationships I've had. I can honestly say it has helped mold me into the person I am today. Yes, I still love my mother. She actually does not live that far from me, approximately an hour. However, there is a huge wall up still. Over the years, we have tried to reconnect. There have been months at a time where we talked and got along, but it always seems like the past creeps up and throws a stumbling block in the way. As of now, we may text once a month, once every two months. Certainly not the relationship I want, but I do hope one day my mom will find the same freedom in Christ that I have. To see her set free and to move on with nothing but forgiveness and a fresh start is what I desire. One thing I have learned in this life, no matter what we have gone through or what kind of relationship we desire with someone, we can only do our part and what God has called us to do. I rest now in the hope that I am obedient to what He may call me to do in restoring my relationship with my mom, and I hope she too will hear God's call.

Now, Jim and I are blessed with nine children—my three

daughters from my first marriage, his two sons and one daughter from previous marriages, twins that Jim and I adopted, and Jim's grandson that we help raise. Throughout the years, Alora, Sarah and Zillah's father has been in and out of their lives. I know my life with him was not the greatest, but I do pray that he will rekindle his love for the Lord and be the man God has called him to be. God saw fit to use him to lead me to His grace. I am grateful for that. I pray that he will be the father that all his kids need. The girls are old enough now to pursue a relationship with their father. My ex and I actually are very cordial with one another today. Holding on to bitterness and reliving the terrifying things of the past keeps you in bondage. But forgiving and moving on sets you on a journey of freedom that is ever so worth it. In the next section of this book, I share with you steps and verses that helped me see where true freedom is.

> "For Brethren, ye have been called unto liberty; only use not liberty for an occasion to the flesh, but by love serve one another. For all the law is fulfilled in one word, even in this; Thou shalt love thy neighbour as thyself"
> (Galatians 5:13-14, KJV).

Think of the one or ones that you are finding it difficult to let go of the hurt you felt from them.

_____

_____

_____

_____

_____

_____

_____

_____

_____

_____

_____

Pray every day for the strength you need to forgive and be set free.

_____

_____

_____

_____

_____

_____

_____

_____

_____

Section 3

Chapter 24: Beginning Your Life in Freedom

The main thing that helped me get past the OCD and negative thinking was understanding the spiritual realms that surround us. Before we go in depth with the spiritual realms, there are a few steps I feel are very important to deal with first. The first step is your salvation. You may have already asked Jesus to be your Savior, if so that was the best choice you could ever make. If not, it really is not that hard. So many think you have to be perfect to come to God, but that is so not true.

To be saved simply means that you trust Jesus as your Savior. We all need saving! Jesus paid the ultimate price so we would not have to go to hell. If you believe that Jesus was born of a virgin birth, that He lived here on earth to show us the way, that He died on the cross, and three days later He rose from the dead, then you are ready for the most life changing experience ever. Now is the time to ask Jesus to forgive you of all your sins, to come into your heart, and be ready to live a life for Him. Yes, it is that simple! If you prayed that prayer, congratulations, you are now a new creation in Christ! You are no longer in darkness, but walking in the light of Jesus. No matter what our lives were before, it does not change who we are now in Christ. I welcome you to the family of God! Some think they have to clean themselves up before making this decision. The true beauty behind that is you don't have to. Come to Jesus just as you are.

Once we acknowledge God and ask Him to forgive and cleanse us, He does!

> "If we confess our sins, he is faithful and just to forgive us of our sins, and to cleanse us from all unrighteousness" *(1 John 1:9, KJV).*

The old you is now gone, but the old habits, thoughts, and actions of your past may continue unless you transform your mind with God's Word. The enemy will come at you throughout life to distract, but applying God's truth, you will overcome.

> "Therefore if any man be in Christ, he is a new creature: old things are passed away; behold, all things are become new"
> *(2 Corinthians 5:17, KJV).*

Chapter 25
Forgiving Others

But, that is not the only forgiving that needs to take place. After securing your salvation in Christ, we need to address forgiveness for others. When we hold unforgiveness against others, it harms us more than them. We are the ones who receive the most benefit from forgiving those that have wronged us. Why forgive others?

• Forgiving others also releases us from bitterness and anger.

• Forgiving helps us to receive the healing we need.

• Holding onto unforgiveness may keep anger built up inside of you.

Although it may be tough to forgive the wrongdoing of someone else, keep in mind what they did to Jesus. On the cross, with love and compassion, Jesus says, "Father forgive them for they know not what they do." What a powerful example. Forgiving does not mean accepting one's sin or wrongdoing. It will release you into experiencing a new joy and freedom.

Matthew 5:44: "But I say unto you, love your ene-
mies, bless them that curse you, do good to them
that hate you, and pray for them which despitefully
use you, and persecute you."
Ephesians 4:31-32: "Let all bitterness, and wrath, and
anger, and clamour, and evil speaking, be put away
from you, with all malice. 32 And be ye kind one to
another, tenderhearted, forgiving one another, even
as God for Christ's sake hath forgiven you."

To experience healing, you must forgive. Forgiveness is a
choice and act of obedience to God. Holding on to the resent-
ment keeps you chained to your past. You may still be hurting,
Jesus knows your hurt. He is here to help you through it. Do not
procrastinate in forgiving. If you want a release from the things
that have kept you bound, forgiving will pave the way.

One mistake that I made over the years was asking God to
help me forgive someone. There is nothing wrong with asking
God for help, but what I was doing was delaying the process by
asking for help and letting God know, "I want to forgive these
people." However, forgiveness is a choice. So, when you forgive someone, let God know that you choose to forgive them.
Choose to forgive. One more example I would like to share is
from [2]Corinthians 2:9-11:

"Don't allow Satan to have an advantage over you.
You are now a child of the most High! And Satan
is under your feet! [10]To whom ye forgive any thing,
I forgive also: for if I forgave any thing, to whom I
forgave it, for your sakes forgave I it in the person of
Christ; [11]Lest Satan should get an advantage of us:
for we are not ignorant of his devices."

Take a few minutes to pray and ask God who are those in your
past or present that need to be forgiven. Be prepared to experience a whole new level of happiness.

Chapter 26
Understanding Fear

Fear is another tactic the enemy will use to keep you from pursuing the life Christ has planned for you. If you are living in fear, or are fearful of things or people, you are not enjoying life.

"There is no fear in love; but perfect love casteth out fear: because fear hath torment. He that feareth is not made perfect in love"
(1 John 4:18, KJV).

What are you afraid of? Know that fear does not come from God. God has given us a stable, courageous mind.

"For God hath not given us the spirit of fear; but of power, and of love, and of a sound mind"
(2 Timothy 1:7, KJV).

One of my favorite definitions of fear is that it is: False Evidence Appearing Real. Satan uses fear to distract us with lies to keep us in a place of not being able to function fully in Spirit. In Matthew, we read of when Jesus walked on the water. Peter asked to walk on water with Jesus. He did. Peter was walking on the water with Jesus. But, when fear set in, Peter began to sink. The fear distracted Peter from what he was doing. He was already walking on the water. Once he let that doubt in, Peter lost his focus.

> "And in the fourth watch of the night Jesus went unto them, walking on the sea. 26 And when the disciples saw him walking on the sea, they were troubled, saying, It is a spirit; and they cried out for fear. 27 But straightway Jesus spake unto them, saying, Be of good cheer; it is I; be not afraid. 28 And Peter answered him and said, Lord, if it be thou, bid me come unto thee on the water. 29 And he said, Come. And when Peter was come down out of the ship, he walked on the water, to go to Jesus. 30 But when he saw the wind boisterous, he was afraid; and beginning to sink, he cried, saying, Lord, save me. 31 And immediately Jesus stretched forth his hand, and caught him, and said unto him, O thou of little faith, wherefore didst thou doubt?"
> *(Matthew 14:25-31, KJV).*

Recognize the fear you have, and take the authority to cast it out. Think on things that are true and good. What God says is truth. Choose faith over fear.

> "Finally, brethren, whatsoever things are true, whatsoever things are honest, whatsoever things are just, whatsoever things are pure, whatsoever things are lovely, whatsoever things are of good report; if there be any virtue, and if there be any praise, think on these things"
> *(Philippians 4:8, KJV).*

Chapter 27
Spiritual Realms

We all live in two different realms. One realm is our natural realm where we can see, smell, and touch things. The other realm is a spiritual realm, the Kingdom of Heaven and the Kingdom of Darkness. These two kingdoms are spiritual realms, usually unseen.

Satan messed up and lost his position in Heaven; now his goal is to get us unfocused and believing his lies. He knows that if he can trap your mind into believing these terrible things about yourself, then you cannot fully operate in the fullness of Christ. There is freedom in Christ and His truth. He came to set us free. My prayer for you is to find freedom and share with others this magnificent truth.

Understanding that there are two spiritual kingdoms, and how they operate will help your steps in freedom.

- In every kingdom there is a ruler or a king, over all.

- These kingdoms must have a realm to where the king can rule.

- Each realm is occupied by citizens.

- You can choose which kingdom to partake in.

- These citizens live by certain customs that were taught to them.

- Each kingdom has strength and power and wants to conquer.

Ephesians 6:12 tells us that the battles we fight are not among ourselves, but against the rulers of Darkness. "For we wrestle not against flesh and blood, but against principalities, against powers, against the rulers of the Darkness of this world, against spiritual wickedness in high places."

Understanding that there is a spiritual realm was the beginning of freedom for me. It helped me take captive the thoughts I was having. Our minds can be a dangerous place. The enemy will attack our minds, making us believe the thoughts he puts there. Unfortunately, he can be very convincing. Not knowing our rightful place in the Kingdom of God will often keep us in bondage to the enemy's lies. When you are facing these trying times and getting lost in your thoughts, it can feel as if it is a real place. At times, you may feel like things are hopeless. From experience, I know how real it is to be lost in the lies and thoughts; it does feel very real. God can bring you to a place to where you don't go by your feelings, but by what you know. However, I encourage you to take your thoughts captive and understand what the enemy is trying to do.

"For though we walk in the flesh, we do not war after the flesh: 4For the weapons of our warfare are not carnal, but mighty through God to the pulling down of

strong holds; [5]Casting down imaginations, and every high thing that exalteth itself against the knowledge of God, and bringing into captivity every thought to the obedience of Christ"
(2 Corinthians 10:3-5, KJV).

Chapter 28
Kingdom of Darkness

First, I want to talk about the Kingdom of Darkness. You may ask yourself, why do we even have the Kingdom of Darkness, and how did this kingdom come about? To begin with, Satan was originally an anointed cherub. He had become rebellious and was no longer to be part of God's Holy Kingdom.

"And he said unto them, I beheld Satan as lightning fall from heaven" *(Luke 10:18, KJV).*

Ezekiel 28:12-19 from the Amplified Bible explains very well what happened.

"[12]Son of man, take up a dirge (funeral poem to be sung) for the king of Tyre and say to him, 'Thus says the Lord God, "You had the full measure of perfection and the finishing touch [of completeness], Full of wisdom and perfect in beauty. [13]"You were in [a] Eden, the garden of God; Every precious stone was your covering: The ruby, the topaz, and the diamond; The beryl, the onyx, and the jasper; The lapis lazuli, the turquoise, and the emerald; And the gold, the workmanship of your [b]settings and your sockets, Was in you. They were prepared On the day that you were created. [14]"You were the anointed cherub who covers and protects, And I placed you there. You were on the holy mountain of God; You walked in the midst of the stones of fire [sparkling jewels]. [15]"You were blameless in your ways From the day you were created Until unrighteousness and evil were found in you. [16]"Through the abundance of your commerce You were internally filled with lawlessness and violence, And you sinned; Therefore I have cast you out as a profane and unholy thing From the mountain of God. And I have destroyed you, O covering cherub, From the midst of the stones of fire. [17]"Your heart was proud and arrogant because of your beauty; You destroyed your wisdom for the sake of your splendor. I cast you to the ground; I lay you before kings, That they might look at you. [18]"You profaned your sanctuaries By the great quantity of your sins and the enormity of your guilt, By the unrighteousness of your trade. Therefore I have brought forth a fire from your midst; It has consumed you, And I have reduced you to ashes on the earth In the sight of all who look at you. [19]"All the peoples (nations) who knew you Are appalled at you; You have come to a horrible and terrifying end And will forever cease to be."

In John 10, the thief mentioned is Satan. This is the plan of the enemy, but read to the end of the verse, and you will see what the plan of God is!

"The thief cometh not, but for to steal, and to kill, and to destroy: I am come that they might have life, and that they might have it more abundantly" *(John 10:10, KJV).*

Satan went to work right away in Genesis, when Eve was in the Garden. When God created man, he had a purpose. God created Adam, then saw fit to give him a helper, Eve. He had given responsibilities and dominion to Adam.

> "So God created man in his own image, in the image of God created he him; male and female created he them. 28And God blessed them, and God said unto them, Be fruitful, and multiply, and replenish the earth, and subdue it: and have dominion over the fish of the sea, and over the fowl of the air, and over every living thing that moveth upon the earth" *(Genesis 1:27-28, KJV).*

God had given instructions to Adam and Eve concerning the garden of Eden. They had access to all the trees in the garden except for one. In Chapter 3, we see how Satan started his work and deceived Eve—resulting in Eve convincing Adam that it was good to eat from the forbidden tree.

> "Now the serpent was more subtil than any beast of the field which the Lord God had made. And he said unto the woman, Yea, hath God said, Ye shall not eat of every tree of the garden? 2And the woman said unto the serpent, We may eat of the fruit of the trees of the garden: 3But of the fruit of the tree which is in the midst of the garden, God hath said, Ye shall not eat of it, neither shall ye touch it, lest ye die. 4And the serpent said unto the woman, Ye shall not surely die: 5For God doth know that in the day ye eat thereof, then your eyes shall be opened, and ye shall

be as gods, knowing good and evil. ⁶And when the woman saw that the tree was good for food, and that it was pleasant to the eyes, and a tree to be desired to make one wise, she took of the fruit thereof, and did eat, and gave also unto her husband with her; and he did eat" *(Genesis 3:1-6, KJV).*

As consequence for all mankind:

"Wherefore, as by one man sin entered into the world, and death by sin; and so death passed upon all men, for that all have sinned" *(Romans 5:12, KJV).*

Satan was named the god of this world.

"In whom the god of this world hath blinded the minds of them which believe not, lest the light of the glorious gospel of Christ, who is the image of God, should shine unto them" *(2 Corinthians 4:4, KJV).*

Resulting in Satan's potion, he does have some power. I remember Jim, my husband now, asking me years ago, why do people that don't follow God do so well in life. God gave this chapter to me to share with him:

"Then was Jesus led up of the Spirit into the wilderness to be tempted of the devil. ²And when he had fasted forty days and forty nights, he was afterward an hungred. ³And when the tempter came to him, he said, If thou be the Son of God, command that these stones be made bread. ⁴But he answered and said, It is written, Man shall not live by bread alone, but by every word that proceedeth out of the mouth of God. [5]Then the devil taketh him up into the holy city, and setteth him on a pinnacle of the temple, [6]And saith unto him, If thou be the Son of God, cast thyself down: for it is written, He shall give his angels charge concerning thee: and in their hands they shall bear thee up, lest at any time thou dash thy foot against a stone. [7]Jesus said unto him, It is written again, Thou shalt not tempt the Lord thy God. [8]Again, the devil taketh him up into an exceeding high mountain, and sheweth him all the kingdoms of the world, and the glory of them; [9]And saith unto him, All these things will I give thee, if thou wilt fall down and worship me. [10] Then saith Jesus unto him, Get thee hence, Satan: for it is written, Thou shalt worship the Lord thy God, and him only shalt thou serve. [11]Then the devil leaveth him, and, behold, angels came and ministered unto him" *(Matthew 4:1-11, KJV).*

We see in verse 9, Satan tells Jesus, "I will give you all these things." Satan will do what he can to try and keep us comfortable. To keep us from knowing we need saving. But, when you come to that place and know that Jesus is here to help you and that the Devil is a liar, you can rest in Matthew 4:11. Having the right mindset and taking the authority that God has given us, you will see the Devil leave and God will send His angels to minister. In Psalm 91:11, God sends His angels to keep us in all our ways. How refreshing is that? God is faithful to keep these promises for you and me. Along with those verses, we also have these amazing promises:

"Ye are of God, little children, and have overcome them: because greater is he that is in you, than he that is in the world" *(1 John 4:4, KJV).*

"Behold, I give unto you power to tread on serpents and scorpions, and over all the power of the enemy: and nothing shall by any means hurt you" *(Luke 10:19, KJV)*.

How can you overcome being a part of the kingdom of darkness? Luke explains it well. In chapter 9, Jesus gathers the twelve disciples, giving them authority and power over all the devils and to cure diseases. Jesus equipped them with what they needed to share the Kingdom of God and to deliver those that were part of the Dark Kingdom.

"Then he called his twelve disciples together, and gave them power and authority over all devils, and to cure diseases. ²And he sent them to preach the kingdom of God, and to heal the sick, ⁶And they departed, and went through the towns, preaching the gospel, and healing every where" *(Luke 9:1-2, 6, KJV)*.

Beginning in chapter 10 of Luke, Jesus explains that the laborers for the Kingdom of God are few and seventy should be sent out to spread the good news of God's Kingdom.

"After these things the Lord appointed other seventy also, and sent them two and two before his face into every city and place, whither he himself would come. ²Therefore said he unto them, The harvest truly is great, but the labourers are few: pray ye therefore the Lord of the harvest, that he would send forth labourers into his harvest" *(Luke 10:1-2, KJV)*.

Keep in mind the demons of the dark kingdom have to obey the voice of those in Christ Jesus!

"¹⁷And the seventy returned again with joy, saying, Lord, even the devils are subject unto us through thy name. ¹⁹Behold, I give unto you power to tread on serpents and scorpions, and over all the power of the enemy: and nothing shall by any means hurt you. ²⁰Notwithstanding in this rejoice not, that the spirits are subject unto you; but rather rejoice, because your names are written in heaven"
(Luke 10:17, 19-20, KJV).

Notice in verse 17, the people were excited about discovering that the devils are subjected to them. They went out and performed what Jesus had told them. Their obedience was in first listening to Jesus, then receiving the power, then being bold and putting what they believe into action. That is our next step! To go out and believe, receive, and have the confidence in the power God has given us through His Son Jesus. We can and we will defeat the Kingdom of Darkness and all the demons that come against us. I strongly believe that understanding these two kingdoms is the beginning of your true freedom.

Chapter 29
The Kingdom of God

Now, let's talk about the Kingdom of God and some of the characteristics of this realm. I can safely assume that this is the kingdom you are pursuing and want to be a citizen of. Which is the best decision you could ever make! Jesus says in John 10:10, "I have come that they may have life, and that they may have it more abundantly." Being a part of the Kingdom of God is being part of a superior, excessive, and superabundant living kingdom!

> "And he said, Whereunto shall we liken the kingdom of God? or with what comparison shall we compare it? 31 It is like a grain of mustard seed, which, when it is sown in the earth, is less than all the seeds that be in the earth: 32 But when it is sown, it groweth up, and becometh greater than all herbs, and shooteth out great branches; so that the fowls of the air may lodge under the shadow of it"
> (*Mark 4:30-32, KJV*).

Several times in scripture, Jesus refers the Kingdom of God as a seed. The Kingdom is planted within us. We should not only be living, but grow and multiply. In God's Kingdom, there is unity! He wants us to be built-up together.

> "Ye also, as lively stones, are built up a spiritual house, an holy priesthood, to offer up spiritual sacrifices, acceptable to God by Jesus Christ" *(1 Peter 2:5, KJV).*

The Kingdom of God is a righteous kingdom. A kingdom full of gifts.

> "For the kingdom of God is not meat and drink; but righteousness, and peace, and joy in the Holy Ghost" *(Romans 14:17, KJV).*

This next verse greatly explains how amazing God's love is for those that choose Him. Those that choose to believe in His goodness and truths. Those that choose to be a citizen of His Kingdom.

> "For he hath made him to be sin for us, who knew no sin; that we might be made the righteousness of God in him" *(2 Corinthians 5:21, KJV).*

Attributes of a righteous person—what we are called to do:
• Reconcile with one another: Matthew 5:22-24
• Keep your word: Matthew 5:37
• Don't seek revenge: Matthew 5:38-42
• Love all unconditionally: Matthew 5:43-48
• Not boastful: Matthew 6:1-4
• Pray from your heart: Matthew 6:5-9
• Forgive others: Matthew 6:14
• Focus on God's goodness: Matthew 6:19-24
• Trust in God: Matthew 6:25-34

- Don't judge: Matthew 7:1-6
- Seeking God in all things: Matthew 7:7-11
- Treat all fairly: Matthew 7:12

Now, don't let this overwhelm you. These are all areas we work on daily. Our Father in Heaven takes us as we are! One misconception that people often have is, they think they need to be perfect and doing all the right things in order to be saved or start a life with Christ. That is wrong. The first step is acknowledging that you need to be saved and asking Jesus into your heart and believing that what He did, He did for you. Trust and believe in what the word of God says. There is so much freedom at your fingertips. I like how this scripture explains our beginning walk with Christ. Daily, we grow.

"And I, brethren, could not speak unto you as unto spiritual, but as unto carnal, even as unto babes in Christ. ²I have fed you with milk, and not with meat: for hitherto ye were not able to bear it, neither yet now are ye able. ³For ye are yet carnal: for where-as there is among you envying, and strife, and divisions, are ye not carnal, and walk as men?"
(1 Corinthians 3:1-3, KJV).

These next verses show the growing process:

"⁶I have planted, Apollos watered; but God gave the increase. ⁷So then neither is he that planteth any thing, neither he that watereth; but God that giveth the increase. ⁸Now he that planteth and he that watereth are one: and every man shall receive his own reward according to his own labour. ⁹For we are labourers together with God: ye are God's husbandry, ye are God's building. ¹⁰According to the

grace of God which is given unto me, as a wise mas-terbuilder, I have laid the foundation, and another buildeth thereon. But let every man take heed how he buildeth thereupon. ¹¹For other foundation can no man lay than that is laid, which is Jesus Christ"
(1 Corinthians 3:6-11, KJV).

God's Kingdom is also a very powerful kingdom.

"And Jesus went about all Galilee, teaching in their synagogues, and preaching the gospel of the king-dom, and healing all manner of sickness and all man-ner of disease among the people. ²⁴And his fame went throughout all Syria: and they brought unto him all sick people that were taken with divers diseases and torments, and those which were possessed with dev-ils, and those which were lunatick, and those that had the palsy; and he healed them"
(Matthew 4:23-24, KJV).

Not only do we have spiritual freedom, but physical free-dom too. When Jesus died on the cross, He died so we could live. He did not die just for us to barely make it, be sick, or tor-mented.

"But he was wounded for our transgressions, he was bruised for our iniquities: the chastisement of our peace was upon him; and with his stripes we are healed"
(Isaiah 53: 5, KJV).

"That it might be fulfilled which was spoken by Esa-ias the prophet, saying, Himself took our infirmities, and bare our sicknesses"
(Matthew 8:17, KJV).

After Jesus rose from the dead, He had given the same powerful freedom to His disciples. Keep in mind, we too are His disciples.

"And when he had called unto him his twelve disciples, he gave them power against unclean spirits, to cast them out, and to heal all manner of sickness and all manner of disease. ⁷And as ye go, preach, saying, The kingdom of heaven is at hand. ⁸Heal the sick, cleanse the lepers, raise the dead, cast out devils: freely ye have received, freely give" *(Matthew 10:1, 7-8, KJV).*

God's Kingdom is a like a treasure, something so precious. This kingdom was created freely for us to enjoy and be free!

"Again, the kingdom of heaven is like unto treasure hid in a field; the which when a man hath found, he hideth, and for joy thereof goeth and selleth all that he hath, and buyeth that field. 45 Again, the kingdom of heaven is like unto a merchant man, seeking goodly pearls: 46 Who, when he had found one pearl of great price, went and sold all that he had, and bought it"
(Matthew 13:44-46, KJV).

"Fear not, little flock; for it is your Father's good pleasure to give you the kingdom" *(Luke 12:32, KJV).*

"Neither shall they say, Lo here! or, lo there! for, behold, the kingdom of God is within you" *(Luke 17:21, KJV).*

This next verse is such a powerful, eye-opening verse!

> "But seek ye first the kingdom of God, and his righ-
> teousness; and all these things shall be added unto
> you"
> *(Matthew 6:33, KJV).*

Chapter 30
Armour of God

Understanding these two kingdoms is not to bring fear upon you, but to help you understand where the attacks come from. Ephesians 6 is a powerful chapter in God's word. It helps explain to us how to prepare for the battle we face. I have heard some say, be sure to put your armour on every morning. Well, I say, be sure not to ever take it off. Once you put your armour on, keep it on!

The armour consists of:
1. The Belt of Truth
2. The Breastplate of Righteousness
3. The Shoes of Peace & Preparation
4. The Shield of Faith
5. The Helmet of Salvation
6. The Sword of The Spirit
7. Prayer, Pray in the Spirit

Before we break down the armor of God, here is the scripture from Ephesians 6:10-20 (KJV).

"[10]Finally, my brethren, be strong in the Lord, and in the power of his might. [11]Put on the whole armour of God, that ye may be able to stand against the wiles of the devil. [12]For we wrestle not against flesh and blood, but against principalities, against powers, against the rulers of the darkness of this world, against spiritual wickedness in high places. [13]Wherefore take unto you the whole armour of God, that ye may be able to withstand in the evil day, and having done all, to stand. [1]Stand therefore, having your loins girt about with truth, and having on the breastplate of righteousness; [15]And your feet shod with the preparation of the gospel of peace; [16]Above all, taking the shield of faith, wherewith ye shall be able to quench all the fiery darts of the wicked. [17]And take the helmet of salvation, and the sword of the Spirit, which is the word of God: [18]Praying always with all prayer and supplication in the Spirit, and watching thereunto with all perseverance and supplication for all saints; [19]And for me, that utterance may be given unto me, that I may open my mouth boldly, to make known the mystery of the gospel, [20]For which I am an ambassador in bonds: that therein I may speak boldly, as I ought to speak."

The first piece of armour is the belt of truth. Truth keeps us secure in Christ. Christ is within you; therefore, the truth is in you too. The truth holds our armour in place.

Psalm 86:11: "Teach me thy way, O Lord; I will walk in thy truth: unite my heart to fear thy name."

John 14:6: "Jesus saith unto him, I am the way, the truth, and the life: no man cometh unto the Father, but by me."

Ephesians 4:25: "Wherefore putting away lying, speak every man truth with his neighbour: for we are members one of another."

John 17:17: "Sanctify them through thy truth: thy word is truth."

The second piece is the breastplate of righteousness. Having this breastplate on gives us the boldness to stand firm in righteous positions in Christ. This breastplate is our defense against the accuser. When he comes at you, you can boldly say that it is not by your own righteousness, but by the righteousness of Christ we are redeemed.

1 Corinthians 1:30: "But of him are ye in Christ Jesus, who of God is made unto us wisdom, and righteousness, and sanctification, and redemption."

Hebrews 4:16: "Let us therefore come boldly unto the throne of grace, that we may obtain mercy, and find grace to help in time of need."

Psalm 94:15: "But judgment shall return unto righteousness: and all the upright in heart shall follow it."

The third piece of armour are the shoes of peace. The shoes God gives send us forth to proclaim the true peace, that is available in Christ. Shoes allow us to step freely without fear. Peacemakers understand the importance of unity. They bring people together in reconciliation.

Romans 10:15: "And how shall they preach, except they be sent? as it is written, How beautiful are the feet of them that preach the gospel of peace, and bring glad tidings of good things!"

Romans 5:1: "Therefore being justified by faith, we have peace with God through our Lord Jesus Christ."

Ephesians 4:3: "Endeavouring to keep the unity of the Spirit in the bond of peace."

Matthew 5:9: "Blessed are the peacemakers: for they shall be called the children of God."

Fourth, we have the shield of faith. A shield is designed to protect a soldier's body during battle. The enemy is out there bombarding us with fiery darts, burning accusations, temptations, and lies. The shield moves with us to stop the attack, no matter what direction the enemy comes from.

Romans 10:17: "So then faith cometh by hearing, and hearing by the word of God."

1 John 5:4: "For whatsoever is born of God overcometh the world: and this is the victory that overcometh the world, even our faith."

Hebrews 11:6: "But without faith it is impossible to please him: for he that cometh to God must believe that he is, and that he is a rewarder of them that diligently seek him."

The next piece of armour is the helmet of salvation. The most critical part of our body is our mind. Satan targets your mind. The weapon he uses are lies. The enemy wants to make us doubt God and our salvation. The helmet protects our minds from doubting the truth of God's word toward us. Be confident and stand firm knowing that our salvation is not based on us, but based on Christ. We cannot ever do enough, but Christ has. Be bold in understanding that nothing can separate you from God and His love.

Romans 8:38-39: "For I am persuaded, that neither death, nor life, nor angels, nor principalities, nor powers, nor things present, nor things to come, 39 Nor height, nor depth, nor any other creature, shall be able to separate us from the love of God, which is in Christ Jesus our Lord."

1 Corinthians 2:16: "For who hath known the mind of the Lord, that he may instruct him? but we have the mind of Christ."

Colossians 1.13: "Who hath delivered us from the power of darkness, and hath translated us into the kingdom of his dear Son."

The sword of the spirit is the next piece of armour. The sword of the spirit is the word of God. God has given us the Bible as a tool to help us understand how to overcome the strongholds, deception, and thoughts that the enemy uses against us. Meditating in this word equips us to recognize and overcome the enemy's tactics.

Romans 10:17: "So then faith cometh by hearing, and hearing by the word of God."

Hebrews 4:12: "For the word of God is quick, and powerful, and sharper than any two-edged sword, piercing even to the dividing asunder of soul and spirit, and of the joints and marrow, and is a discerner of the thoughts and intents of the heart."

2 Timothy 3:16: "All scripture is given by inspiration of God, and is profitable for doctrine, for reproof, for correction, for instruction in righteousness."

Now we have the protective power of prayer to keep at all times. Prayer is simply communicating with God. There is no right or wrong way to do it. All you have to do is talk with Him. As we desire to have those conversations with our spouse or best friend, that is how God is. He desires us to be ourselves and confidently come to Him. Prayer is not always asking God for something, but you can naturally just tell Him how beautiful the sky is. I look at the sky as paintings from my Father. He sure does know how to paint some beautiful pictures. Make a habit of greeting God first thing in the morning, and talk with Him throughout the day.

> *1 Thessalonians 5:16-18:* "Rejoice evermore. [17]Pray without ceasing. [18]In every thing give thanks: for this is the will of God in Christ Jesus concerning you."

> *Philippians 4:6-7:* "Be careful for nothing; but in every thing by prayer and supplication with thanksgiving let your requests be made known unto God. [7]And the peace of God, which passeth all understanding, shall keep your hearts and minds through Christ Jesus."

> *Matthew 21:22:* "And all things, whatsoever ye shall ask in prayer, believing, ye shall receive."

With confidence, put your armour of God on. Be bold in who you have been called to be! You are a child of the most High! Throughout the Bible, you will also see other scriptures referring to having this armour on.

> *1 Thessalonians 5:8:* "But let us, who are of the day, be sober, putting on the breastplate of faith and love; and for an helmet, the hope of salvation."

> *2 Corinthians 10:3-6:* "For though we walk in the flesh, we do not war after the flesh: [4](For the

weapons of our warfare are not carnal, but mighty through God to the pulling down of strong holds;) ⁵Casting down imaginations, and every high thing that exalteth itself against the knowledge of God, and bringing into captivity every thought to the obedience of Christ; 6 And having in a readiness to revenge all disobedience, when your obedience is fulfilled."

Isaiah 59:17: "For he put on righteousness as a breastplate, and a helmet of salvation upon his head; and he put on the garments of vengeance for clothing, and was clad with zeal as a cloak."

Chapter 31: Maintaining Your Christian Walk

One important step in maintaining your walk with Christ is taking your thought life captive. If you do not control the way you think, your mind can cause you to drift. One verse that shed light on the struggles of my thought life was in Matthew 6:27. "Which of you, by taking thought, can add one cubit unto his stature?"

That verse had me thinking. Can you add height to your stature just by thinking? No matter what anxious thoughts I had, they were not going to come true just by having that thought. So many get caught up in fear, fearing the thoughts that come to their minds. Just because Satan puts a thought in your head, does not make it real. Getting to know the truths and promises in God's word will also help you overcome the battle that happens in your mind. You will learn to transfer the negative thoughts over to the delightful promises that God has promised you.

Something I want you to think about is relationships. You remember how it was when you were dating, and you couldn't wait to talk to your boyfriend or girlfriend. You were excited to see them and go out on dates. Hopefully, if you are married, you still have that exciting bond with your spouse. Now, think about God. How do you want your relationship to be with Him? How do you think He wants your relationship with Him to be? He desires the same kind of relationship with you that you do with the ones you love. He too wants to have date nights with you, long walks on the beach, picnics, and just your everyday casual conversations. He wants to be your best friend. The more time you spend with Him, the more you will get to know who He is.

Reading His word is very important. I look at the Bible as someone going into the military. One of the first things soldiers do is go through boot camp. They get their instructions and learn how to use the equipment they need to fight in the war they are getting ready to face. The same is true with Christians. As you read in Ephesians, you see that we are in a spiritual battle. The word of God helps equip us with what we need to overcome the battles. Jesus came to be an example for us. Getting to know Jesus, will also give you an understanding of the Father's love for us. Starting with the New Testament—Matthew, Mark, Luke and, John—all four books tell the account of Jesus's life from the perspective of each author. When I took the time to read those four books, it helped me to see who Jesus really is.

The Bible can be hard to understand, especially for beginners. You can get involved in study groups or get Bible study books. I like the Amplified Bible as well when it comes to understanding what the scriptures are saying. The amplified version breaks each verse up and gives a more detailed description of what is being said.

Prayer is very important in one's Christian walk. 1Thessalonians 5:17 says, "Pray without ceasing." Prayer simply means talking to God. It is a great way to build your relationship and communication with Him. I like to start each morning out with greeting God. Sometimes it is very short and just a simple, "Good morning Lord." Sometimes I go into more detail. I will walk outside and compliment God on the beauty that I see. I have even asked God to help me with my hair and what to wear. I believe God smiles and adores when we include Him in the simplest things. At times in my prayer time, I like to be completely silent. As a woman, that can be really hard, but I do it. I want to hear and receive from Him. God cares about every area of our life. No matter how big or how small it may seem. Pray without ceasing. Talk to God all day, every day!

Worship is so very powerful. Worshipping God means to honor and have reverence for Him. It is also an expression of adoration for our Father. There is no right or wrong way to worship! For me, I love to put on some praise music and go running. That is some of my quiet time that I spend with the Lord. Other times, I sit and listen to praise music. I also like to have it playing throughout the day. Yes, at times I dance around the kitchen worshipping and getting lost in His goodness. Worship leads you into the presence of God. Sometimes, I will play a song and just rest to enter into His presence.

"God is a Spirit: and they that worship him must worship him in spirit and in truth" *(John 4:24, KJV)*.

I believe that you should take the time to read, pray, and worship with the Lord daily. Doing these things will help your relationship with God grow stronger and deeper.

As you may struggle with the insecurities that the enemy has lied to you about over the years, I have made up this list of 'I AM's' that you can declare over your life daily! I encourage you to make a copy and post this list in a place where you will see it every day.

I AM holy - 1 Peter 1:16
I AM righteous - 1 John 3:7
I AM redeemed - Ephesians 1:7

I AM forgiven - Colossians 1:13,14
I AM loved - John 3:16
I AM heir - Romans 8:17
I AM rescued - Hebrews 13:6
I AM victorious - 1 John 5:4
I AM justified - Romans 5:1
I AM accepted - Ephesians 1:6
I AM blessed - Ephesians 1:3
I AM blameless - 2 Peter 3:14
I AM sealed - 2 Corinthians 1:22
I AM bold - Ephesians 6:19
I AM complete - Colossians 2:9-10
I AM chosen - John 15:16
I AM anointed - 1 John 2:27
I AM healed - Isaiah 53:5
I AM courageous - Psalms 27:14
I AM worthy - Colossians 1:10
I AM cleansed - 1 John 1:7
I AM restored - Psalm 23:3
I AM protected - Psalm 91:7
I AM beautiful - Genesis 1:27
I AM set apart - Psalm 4:3
I AM a friend - John 15:15
I AM renewed - Psalm 51:10
I AM legitimate - Romans 8:30
I AM strong - Philippians 4:13
I AM a conqueror - Romans 8:37
I AM alive - Ephesians 2:4-5
I AM saved - Ephesians 2:8-9
I AM sanctified - 1 Thessalonians 5:23
I AM delivered - Psalms 50:15
I AM an overcomer - 1 John 5:5
I AM confident - Proverbs 14:26
I AM prosperous - Psalms 1:3

I am excited for you to embrace these truths from God's word. You are an overcomer and the victory is yours! My prayer for you is to have the courage to share this freedom with others. Your story is a story that needs to be heard and may be the beginning of freedom for someone else. Never lose sight of who you are in Christ! Be bold and confident as you walk with the Lord. Be blessed, my friend, and know that you are loved!

> "Beloved, I wish above all things that thou mayest prosper and be in health, even as thy soul prospereth"
> *(3 John 1:2, KJV).*

Please feel free to reach out to me. I know how difficult and overwhelming the struggle of overcoming can be.

You can find me on Facebook at:
Lutricia Lopez-Author of Younger Me: You are Free

Email me at <u>lutricialopez.youarefree@gmail.com</u>

CPSIA information can be obtained
at www.ICGtesting.com
Printed in the USA
BVHW03s0442230418
513861BV00001B/37/P